Against Urbanism

Franco La Cecla

*Translated from the Italian
by Mairin O'Mahony*

the
**green
arcade**

Against Urbanism
Franco La Cecla. Translated by Mairin O'Mahony
© 2020 PM Press

The materials contained in this book are the fruit of studies undertaken, over the past years, by Franco La Cecla for the Research Laboratory on Cities (Laboratorio di ricerca sulle città) at the University of Bologna.

ISBN: 978-1-62963-235-3
Library of Congress Control Number: 2016948159

Cover art by Gent Sturgeon
Cover layout by John Yates / www.stealworks.com
Interior design by briandesign

10 9 8 7 6 5 4 3 2 1

PM Press
PO Box 23912
Oakland, CA 94623
www.pmpress.org

The Green Arcade
1680 Market Street
San Francisco, CA 94102–5949
www.thegreenarcade.com

Printed in the USA.

Contents

CHAPTER 1

The Return of the Body to the City

OVER THE COURSE OF THE LAST YEARS I HAVE BECOME A witness to an unexpected transformation that I never imagined would happen. The first time it happened was in Cairo, the second was in Istanbul, and the third was in Hong Kong. In Cairo I had participated in a seminar organized by the NGO Liveinslums in the City of the Dead,[1] the district that is the monumental cemetery for the city, inhabited today by over half a million people who, thanks to an ingenious system of overbuilding, have created within, above and around the tombs, a close-knit and tranquil habitat (compared with the rest of the city). On that occasion the city appeared immense and completely blocked in a huge anxiety, so that it seemed impossible to have any kind of discourse with the people that would touch on the hope of the minutest change. It was the last year of Mubarak's government, but we did not know that.

Back home again in Italy, we were overcome by events. It appeared to us that a city from which all representative spaces had been removed suddenly became the protagonist in an immense revolt against the central power. Contrary to what the Cairene intellectuals who were interviewed had to tell us, here was no fragmented opposition which had finally gathered some courage, but rather an immense and orderly crowd, identifying itself with a space, Tahrir Square. During those days in the streets, a good friend and a great moviemaker, Stefano Savona, found himself in Cairo. And he understood that something unique was taking place, and with a minimum amount of equipment he installed himself in Tahrir Square with the occupiers. Wrapped in a shower curtain taken from his room in the nearby hotel, he slept with them and saw for himself the waiting, the outside attacks, the long resistance. And he filmed the protagonists, showing their faces and their bodies, creating in my opinion something totally unforeseen: photographing a revolution up close, where every participant was a protagonist.

It was a technique made possible by the equipment Stefano was using, blending in with the crowd and filming them body to body, but above all it was a discourse about what was happening. Here one was involved not just with a demonstration in the streets, but with the notion that to combat power it needed the people, young and old, entire families and students, Muslims and Copts, Islamic organizations and laypeople inspired by Che Guevara, poets and singers, people who blog and people who don't, to occupy a place physically. I visited the square and it seemed to me to be one of the dustiest and most anonymous of places in the city, important only because it is central and a couple of steps away from the seats of power. Today it has become Tahrir Square, a place that brings together the most disparate components and unites them in the idea that change cannot happen on Facebook or elsewhere on the internet, but only in the physical presence of millions of bodies in the streets. It is this occupation of the streets that created identity, constituted a new subject and proposed an idea of a citizenry with the right to be present together in a public space. There is a moment in Stefano Savona's film *Tahrir: Revolution Square*, the one that he made and distributed right after the events, in which a girl in a hijab contacts one of the protest leaders on Facebook.[2] He doesn't want to come to the demonstration because he thinks it is being led by the Muslim Brotherhood, but she reassures him that no, it is everyone and above all the many who want the downfall of Mubarak and a new constitution. It's an important moment, because we understand that something completely unexpected is happening that the devotees of the web have not cottoned to. What is novel is the taking back of the centrality of the connection between urban people and urban spaces, their right to exercise their own presence in the public spaces of the city, a gesture and a practice that puts back into play the physicality of the city and of its citizens.

A Norwegian anthropologist, Unni Wikan, who has worked for forty years straight in Cairo among the poor of the city, had foreseen something similar. She had understood that the international organizations, preoccupied with the transformation of Cairo into a sustainable city, were completely unaware of the daily experiences of the inhabitants. During the nineties, the United Nations organization that had asked for a consultation with the anthropologist concluded that conditions in the city were worsening. Wikan, however, concluded the opposite: that there were citizens' networks of solidarity, which were working together day by day to provide a better future for their own children, making informal and illegal work arrangements by making deals with the owners of vacant lots to provide construction materials and building work in exchange for long-term leases, effectively providing a co-responsibility that enhanced the lives of everyone concerned. The problem for Wikan was that these processes were invisible to the international organizations, invisible precisely because they were dependent on the delicate tissue of the daily give-and-take in the physical presence of the people of the neighborhood. So when the millions in the streets went from being invisible to visible all of a sudden, the "urgent and necessary" work (here Wikan uses the binomial phrase coined by Pierre Bourdieu to describe the everyday condition of the poor) of the Cairenes to ameliorate the condition of life for the next generations slips under the radar and is not noticed. Wikan had intuited that anthropology as a discipline was blind with respect to the urban poor, and that the urban planner was incapable of understanding how people were using and occupying the spaces in their own city with an eye to improving their everyday life: "It is not coincidental that the urban poor of the Third World remain peripheral to the anthropological scene: they don't have much to offer us that is exotic. They don't use fancy words, or recite poetry, or engage in elaborate rituals. In fact, as E.V. Walter notes, 'The poor have plenty, but it is plenty of what nobody wants.'"[3]

Wikan's report was turned down and attacked as irrelevant. She was forced to publish it elsewhere so that it might gain visibility and have an effect.[4] What happened in Tahrir Square is the same type of phenomenon. Accustomed as we are to think that changes happen "online" or on a global scale, we do not take into account that they are made by human beings in urban spaces and that the mere presence of people in the streets taking back their own right to the city is an explosive political reality.

This can be seen in the events that followed the fall of Mubarak. The streets have determined a good part of the evolution or of the political regression of the Egyptian Spring. (But in our idea of "the streets" there is a negative political judgment: the streets would be the subconscious collective, incapable of emerging from barbarism.) They are the place where the opposition was constructed and destructed and reconstructed, where the destiny of the Muslim Brotherhood and of the secular Egypt which wasn't there were played out, where military repression was unleashed, along with the successful attempt at a new coup d'état. Yet Tahrir Square is very frightening to the new regime, who have in fact rendered it almost inaccessible. Because it is there that one can sense the radical difference between the opposition parties and the religious movements. How true it is that the same Muslim Brotherhood, who attempted to ride in on the revolt in Tahrir Square, was thrown from the saddle, precisely because it did not recognize that the city was expressing itself in the streets as a complex and composed structure, refusing to be identified as not belonging to that city and to that square and to those streets.

This new concept of citizenship threw me for a loop a second time in Istanbul. It's a city which I had begun visiting regularly and which also seemed to me to be "stuck." I felt the discontent in the attitude of my artist and actor friends who had brought me to a demonstration of solidarity with the pianist Fazil Say,[5] threatened with exile because he had posted a tweet in which he criticized the muezzin in his neighborhood, where, the pianist said, "not only am I an atheist, but I also have to put up with the muezzin who is off-key!" At that demonstration in a theater in Beyoğlu there was a motley opposition that didn't react adequately to the belief that Erdoğan wants to get into one's private life in order to control it. It seemed to me to have something to do with an old Left a little too radical and nostalgic to understand such a complex country. Still, a few months later Gezi Park exploded. And even here, who could have predicted that a place in the city, a place that is pretty well anonymous, an awkwardly placed urban hub with an overhead garden, would become the symbol of the "taking back" of the city by its citizens? Everyone poured out into the streets here, poor people and middle-class, young and old, Kemalists nostalgic for Atatürk and progressive Sufis, veiled and nonveiled women, artists, workers, people of every stripe. The new version of citizenship emerged here even regardless of the generally accepted pretext that says that the only important things are changes on the web. Cairo and Istanbul teach us that the peculiarity of urban revolt revolves around a retake on the concept of citizenship as physical presence. Gezi Park lasted for many months, with injuries and fatalities, with a fascist police force shooting at human height level and using a very dangerous, illegal, and irritating poison gas. It spread to Ankara and Izmir and throughout a good part of Turkey.

When I went back to Istanbul (a year had passed since Gezi Park) I got caught up in an encounter between the police and the demonstrators.[6] It took place in the Cihangir quarter of Beyoğlu with the demonstrators showing their slogan "Cihangir is ours" on one side and the police in full riot gear on the other. This confrontation happened every evening for a week, in spite of, it should be pointed out, the liberticide laws passed by Erdoğan forbidding every form of assembly, these still happened as an expression of the right to be citizens in their own city, a "physical" right, the presence of their bodies. The demonstrators responded to the tear gas canisters by tossing fireworks, a turn in the demonstration that in those days had taken on an ever more theatrical aspect. To the Erdoğan prohibition against assembly the citizens of the community were simply "standing" in Gezi Park to read the newspaper or simply to make it known that they were "resisting" (a move invented by choreographer Erdem Gündüz, who had first demonstrated that way in the streets). This conduct overturned the old method of demonstrating and marching. And it touched on the weak point of the new neoliberal tyranny in full swing around the world: not being able to stand that citizens are "using" their city and not using it up. It is the unpredictability of this usage that upsets the old and new tyrannies. James C. Scott, an anthropologist concerned with resistance and the establishment of forms of opposition forces, has explored the extent of these phenomena.[7] There is a method of resisting the State that shows itself by inhabiting places. Just living, if it is not a contraction of daily life in private spaces, in a residential setting, is a form of political resistance.

Now that Erdoğan has become president "for life," things will undoubtedly become much worse, but what has happened in Istanbul and in Turkey tells us that there is a transformation of outlook on a monumental scale. Now, if citizens of Kurdish origin wish to demonstrate against the hypocrisy of Erdoğan, whose army which is deployed against Isis on the border with Syria, lets the Kurdish peshmerga be massacred and does not intervene, so the public spaces on the streets return to the limelight. It seems that Erdoğan will have to scale back his real estate pretensions (his brother owns the largest real estate company in the country and has the contract for the better part of all public works). The citizens have understood that it is in the urban geography of public spaces that the future of Erdoğan and of their country will be played out.

Finally, the streets and the body of citizens have surfaced on the scene in a place where it might have least been expected, in one of the centers of new Asian capitalism, Hong Kong, which for over twenty years has "returned" to become part of China, but with a relatively independent autonomy.

Precisely to defend the right to this autonomy, students, young people who do not identify with the ideas practiced by their parents, came out into the streets to block the most important sectors of the city: Admiralty, Central, Montgomery, Mong Kok. What most bothered those who wished that the students be evicted was to see an anomalous use of the streets and of the few public spaces. The students slept in the middle of the cross streets which at the best of times are congested and crawling with cars. We are talking about something quite different from a functioning traffic system. They transformed a hectic city where "money is made" into stasis, in the Greek sense, that is, into a space for political transformation. It is irritating for the government of Hong Kong and for Beijing when the image of the way of life of the financial center does not correspond with the image of a world city. It's the result of a much more complicated lifestyle which allows a populated city, to have at the same time a stratification for "the rich" and a relative space for autonomous growth. At base is the idea that Hong Kong is and remains an island, an oasis of comparatively liberal thinking, of art, cinema, music, but above all, of free and open behavior. Here one doesn't settle for the web, even if the organization of the occupation was done through tweets, in spite of the government's efforts to block sites and stop tweets, which were met with the usual creativity and channel-switching and encryptions. Even in Istanbul the web served to "counter-geolocate" the presence of the demonstrators, to facilitate speedy and immediate getaways, and to spread in real time what was happening in the streets.

Hong Kong demonstrates that cities have a concrete function, that of allowing new citizens to gather themselves together and to send a strong message of the "desultoriness" with regard to the normative functioning of the capitalist city. The declarations of the demonstrators after three weeks of occupation and the violent interventions by the police followed by the logic of the disbandment after negotiation are abundantly clear. The occupations of the streets will continue because they give the power of negotiation to the students, who know only too well how difficult it will be to convince the Chinese government to concede more autonomy. But obviously on the table it is the theatricalization of urban space in the forefront of world attention and the symbolic aspect of the young bodies who refuse to back down before the obvious functionality of Hong Kong. If it were not such a hackneyed thought, one might talk of biopolitics in opposition. Today power is not just power over people; whatever means people use to resist power is also a power. And there is an anti-Debord dramatics about the way the response to the mace sprayed by the police was a display of umbrellas. That has a symbolic weight far beyond any actual functionality. But it's difficult to convey this to those who see one as "leftist," as according to the parameters of the New Left it was merely the youthful caprices of yobboes wanting to take selfies.

Today there are "big cities" and often their "nonplaces," which urban planners, sociologists, and anthropologists consider to be absolutely anonymous, so as to display a political method different from what they are. In the fiction of the new tyrannies there is an empty city and it is administered by the paranoia of an urban planner who is preoccupied with separating, zoning, controlling, closing off the rich and the middle classes in gated communities, and shutting off the slums behind metal screens. On the other hand, the urban poor and even the lower class and the middle class know that now, as never before, the city is an indefeasible resource, precisely because it is in the everyday nature of its spaces, private or public, that they are able to exercise the capacity for ameliorating their way of life.

It is interesting that the urban planner today reveals his conceptual poverty in light of these changes. More than any other human science, urban planning is incapable of taking into account its own paradigms, of renewing itself. It is incapable because it has epistemologically lost the sense of reality. Planners barricade themselves in and hide behind statistics, maps, trends, and flows and are unable to enter into the physical life of the people with regard to the physical aspect of places in the city. In this cascade of implements, in this intellectual poverty, there is the end of a discipline that has settled behind the defense lines of a blind technicality and has never wanted to become a "human science." Twenty-five years have passed since I wrote about urban planning in an essay called *L'urbanistica é una scienza umana?* [Is City Planning a Human Science?][8] in which I demonstrated its profound inhumanity. Town planning is incapable of knowing what is happening in cities because it is closed off between numeric parameters and "lists," because it believes that social reality is transferable into mapping and percentages and calculations of probabilities. It is obvious that real movements and real motivations, what the people who live in a city think and feel about it and the motivation that it gives them for living there, are being sidestepped. If the real-life components of the citizenry at every level, from the poor to the middle classes, to the urban rich, are not understood, if one doesn't get the logic of belonging to places, one cannot grasp what is happening or could be happening.

Anthropology is an essential instrument only if it bases itself on the criterion that Unni Wikan hoped for. It has more to do with reading and not the culture of the people (a terminology dear to anthropology that has ended up disguising human immanence) but rather of the experience lived in town. And this dimension, that of the lived experience which I have defined elsewhere as "local mind,"[9] and the interlacing of living and locations in a reciprocal daily construction of identity. Anthropology can help urban planners to renew themselves, but first this outdated and useless discipline needs to be razed to the ground in order to be put back on its feet. The problem is that it continues to be the bailiwick of the privileged sucking up to the palaces of power, be they tyrants or international organizations. As long as urban planning resembles a discipline of police policies for cities, as long as it has a prescriptive character, it will be impossible for it to assume new ears and eyes and become first and foremost a discipline to which cities pay attention.

NOTES

1   Liveinslums, www.liveinslums.org.

2   *Tahrir: Liberation Square*, directed by Stefano Savona (Dugong and Picofilms, 2011).

3   Unni Wikan, *Resonance: Beyond the Words* (Chicago: University of Chicago Press, 2014), 71.

4   Unni Wikan, "Sustainable Development in the Mega-City: Can the Concept Be Made Applicable?," *Current Anthropology* 36, no. 4 (1995): 635–55.

5   "Turkey: Fazil Say Contemplates Exile, 'Insulted as Atheist,'" ANSAmed, April 23, 2012, http://www.ansamed.info/ansamed/en/news/sections/culture/2012/04/23/Turkey-Fazil-Say-contemplates-exile-insulted-atheist-_6764811.html.

6   Franco La Cecla, "Turchia News," October 11, 2013, www.alfabeta2.it/2013/10/11/turchia-news.

7   James C. Scott, *Domination and the Arts of Resistance: Hidden Transcripts* (New Haven, CT: Yale University Press, 1990).

8   Franco La Cecla, "L'urbanistica è una scienza umana?," *Urbanistica*, no. 106 (1996).

9   Franco La Cecla, *Mente locale*, preface by P.K. Feyerabend (Milan: Eleuthera, 2008).

CHAPTER 2

Images of Cities

The private moment and the public moment are not next to each other like a bedroom and a doctor's consulting room but are interwoven with one another. When the most private act takes place publicly, even public things are decided in private, and so entail a physical political responsibility, which is something completely different from the metaphoric and moral. The private person assumes the responsibility for public acts, because he is always on the spot.

—Walter Benjamin[1]

OFTEN WHEN I AM GETTING TO KNOW A NEW CITY, ambling along its streets, taking the bus to the end of the line, mixing with the people buying noodles, standing in line for a *parota* in Allahabad in India or for a *nasi goreng* in Penang in Malaysia, mingling in the markets and in the temples, I have thought: "I could live here!" A whimsical thought that maybe comes because I am an anthropologist, or maybe it's the opposite, the intimate desire to discover for myself what it's like to belong to a place, is what led me to anthropology. The fact is that for me this was a surprise. I discovered it the first time in Tashkent in Uzbekistan, a place I arrived in by chance, and it has happened many other times in spite of myself.

There are cities about which I have heard bad things or cities about whose existence I knew nothing or cities that I could never picture myself involved in. But I don't have a preconceived idea of them, and suddenly a revelation will invite me to step into the shoes of those who live there. Sometimes this prime impulse will lead me to make an experiment, to stay in that city, until I feel a little like one of its inhabitants, until I can't move away from the center, until I know the seasons and can slip slowly into unawareness that what was once so new has become everyday, and you have the feeling of being part of a shared world, a world made of houses, spaces, trees, rain, moon, and burning sun or refreshing breezes. And this desire to know how those others are living pushes me to spy on them and to behave like them and to remain for a good part of the time in mystery. What would it be like in Singapore? How would it be to try Istanbul? What kind of pride or fearfulness would I get living in a provincial city like Jogjakarta in Java or like Penang in Malaysia? In Vietnam at a certain point I understood the pride of being from Hanoi, the northern identity which is still caught between a sense of guilt regarding the south and the pride of having saved the country, the idea of being a little too "Chinese," and therefore not true Viet descendants of the Champa who came from India, as did the southerners. I felt that mix of rationality and at the same the "Naples-ness" of Hanoi.[2]

But it has happened to me on other occasions, this desire to get into the experience of living in a city, of pretending to belong there. It is an experience that has always led to frustration but has also strengthened the security of my attachment to Palermo, to the fact that I am so well aware of an extremely provincial city's pretentious sense of centrality yet proud to be a part of it. In general, however, the experience of "living" in a city has nothing to do with a more or less moral judgment on how one lives there. Instead it's to do with envy of those who are *insiders* and not *outsiders*. How we envy those Istanbulites moving around in their immense city on the Bosporus! How we envy the inhabitants of the Bay Area and San Francisco and their gift of being faced by the whole cosmopolitan world that surrounds them. How we envy the inhabitants of the *mahalle* of Tashkent in Uzbekistan their security in living in a compound apparently made of mud but tiled with marble on the inside. I think that this is the mainspring of my travels, trying to understand how it feels "on the inside," how it would be to be a real inhabitant of the place. Obviously it is an experiment in impossibility, even if the desire brings us closer to a valuable intuition, even if one could come to feel like the "locals," experience the "resonance" talked about by Unni Wikan. It is possible to resonate, to harmonize even, with people whose language one does not understand but whose way of living one observes, even if they are people with different religions, cultures and customs.

This experience passes for the sharing of everyday nature, for abandoning the oddity of arriving from the outside, to share food, drinks, daytimes and nighttimes, daily rhythms and body movements. In resonance, in harmony, it is our body that first learns and then explains, without our being aware of it, what it is like to be "in place," in the physical imitation of the other bodies which are living there for some time, long before us. When you live in a place you adapt to its motions; there are cities that lead one to walk with a muffled tread, such as Venice, cities such as New York in which a kind of nervousness seizes one's legs and drives you on, cities where sweat and humidity teach you different rhythms; there are cities where you learn to move your limbs like them, the natives, to make the same grimaces that they make, gestures to get you into the part, as in Naples or Mumbai. Bodies are shaped by the cities in which they live, by their steps or flat areas, by their ascents and declines, by the grassy areas and by the dust. I don't know whether this is anthropology, but it is certainly a part of alienation and of putting oneself into another world, part of the magnificent temptation to pretend to be somebody else. Anthropology is a form of knowledge of disguise; as Tim Ingold says, "Anthropology is the philosophy with the courage to live outside."[3]

Lurking behind our admiration for—or our terror of—the web, there is in this return to the body a renewal of something that up to now seemed on the way to extinction or already extinct forever. It is that nucleus which for Lewis Mumford constituted the sense of the city, that contiguous corporality which was founded in the Greek polis and continued up to the preindustrial Gothic city. For Mumford, the "culture of the city" was the human experiment of living together that produced arts and crafts, guilds and trade, the Greek isonomy and the Renaissance city-states.[4] The culture of the city was vis-à-vis, a primary relationship between people and spaces, corners of walls and bell towers, neighbors across the street and seamen, arcades and temples, merchants and washerwomen. But as time went on life had to be redefined in London, Paris, and Rome, in the first hiccups of New York and Chicago.

Even in the years between the two wars, when Saint Petersburg became Leningrad, or in the San Francisco of the Gold Rush, one still lived with the dialectic of friends and passersby. The city was a place of arriving, staying, and leaving, a place which owed its existence to the coexistence of people among people, even with the acceleration of the Industrial Revolution, the day-to-day activities resulted in the essential functioning of society. Cities were shaken by wars, and then came the most potent war against them, declared by the empire of rubber-tired traffic: the conservative and reactionary revolution of the individual automobile. The elementary dimension stopped. Replaced by favored ropes, wires, visible and invisible connections, images and voices in transition and movement. The cities have been deconstructed until they are almost totally dis-incarnated. Who could be interested any more in the existence of historical centers, attentive to the subtle nuances of their being, who could care about porticoes and stairways, promenades and covered passages? They are part of an archaeological past to be entrusted to little old ladies interested in old walls. For the urban planner it was time for the discovery of conservation. The duty to defend the antique, knowing full well what it means to be realists, of defending the walls but not their long-past functions. Whoever would build for a coexistence between houses and shops? Who would have struck a blow for a real centrality in the old centers? Up to now the suburbs, the commercial centers and the freeways were the true places where life was happening. Then Europe was invaded by immigrants from other worlds. And these people began to use the city with their bodies, to use them to make a primary resource of their spaces. Precisely because they were exiled from their own places of origin, it was the spatiality of the city in which they had arrived which was able to offer them the conquest of new worlds.[5] In Riccardo Arena's beautiful novel *La letteratura tamil a Napoli* one can understand this new original reality, where the old and new physicalities are superimposed.[6]

In the centers of the old European cities they have created places for making phone calls, for sending money, pop-up retail spaces, hairdressers, "oriental" fast food. We have discovered the immigrants while they are appropriating the spaces that we find too obsolete or by now too awkward even for parking. We would never have imagined that the day would come when we would be asking ourselves how we overlooked the possibilities of these same places. Cities, having become the abstract sites of our residences, are getting away from us. And with that distancing, the possibility of direct democracy, the everyday quality of life, and the pretext of belonging ourselves are also getting away. Through the existence of the immigrants we are slowly discovering our own existence. However, we have had to bring ourselves to the time of the occupations, to the presence of occupiers in Tahrir Square, Gezi Park, Mong Kok, but also on Wall Street, the streets of Brazil, occupations of our cities full of empty and underused buildings, to acknowledge that dis-incarnation is undermining our cities, draining them of meaning and rendering assemblies useless. The body is returning to center stage, with its demands and its postures, its rhythms and its avoidances. The senses are returning to center stage, the art of living and moving, bodies among bodies, and the art of avoiding each other. Today we are on the verge of either a rediscovery or completely losing both city and body. Because cities are the theater of bodies and are the scene where they can play out with the limited and powerful strength that they have, the strength of those with "staying power."

Jogjakarta, Java, Indonesia

These Indonesian cities are strange: they seem like a spread of temporary shanties with every now and then a reinforced-concrete shopping mall. I walk around Jogjakarta, a medium-sized place (one million eight hundred thousand inhabitants) and I ask myself what holds a city like this together? I encounter thousands of eyes and limbs, and the Indonesian mix is startling, here in the main street of Malioboro, which is the Portobello Road of Jogja, as the Indonesians call it. Scooters, cars, horse-drawn carriages, and the local rickshaws. The answer is that it is commerce that holds this city together. There are huge markets open to the skies, enormous markets that sell everything you can imagine, from batik in every price range to headgear of every type, from "snakeskin" fruit to electronics. You get the feeling here that cities are responding to the exigency of finding themselves on the spot where the merchandise converges. The residential section is off to one side. But then it is enough to thread one's way into the maze of little streets which branch off from the main drag of Malioboro to find oneself in front of a little building, little houses with tiny gardens and roofs like a witch's hat which recall what the city must have been like before independence. It's difficult for a westerner to puzzle out this phenomenon, the Indonesian "made-up" city. But it's a good exercise to try. It pushes me to ask myself what exactly constitutes cities? Here there are enormous movements of collective groups which move around and congregate. And depending on the time of day they take up different positions on the ground. On their scooters are the young girls, wearing the hijab or with their hair blowing in the wind or under a helmet and the rest of the crowd is on foot, squashing in and brushing up against one another. A compact crowd, different from one in Mumbai or Cairo. A crowd pushed more toward middle-class, with fewer beggars and fewer homeless people sleeping on the sidewalks. But then by the evening everything changes, the crowd that during the day was moving around is now occupying the sidewalk, sitting cross-legged or stretched out on mats to sample fried bebek, *the local crackling duck, or other tasty spicy treats like* warung, *bought from the street food vendors in their ramshackle booths. One has to eat something on the street, and for the young people of the city it's a kind of ritual, a symbol of something, and they bring their guitars and sing long into the night. The density of the group in the night is still startling, even with the softening of the noise, but here, unlike India, one hardly every hears car horns. What does the city mean here? I ask myself once more. The answer is the buses that take people from here to Borobudur, which is a shrine for national pilgrimage, or the ones that cross Java to the east. The answer is the station, around which is a labyrinth of alleys, the souk which offers economical lodgings to the backpackers, and to the locals, a brothel of immense proportions, with girls of all ages, sad-eyed and bored in the smoky corners and the yellowish atmosphere of their private rooms. It seems a little bit like a shantytown. But in reality, that's a mistaken impression. Because we're not talking here about cardboard lean-tos but of an* Existenzminimum *which enjoys the realization that in Indonesian cities the doors and windows always remain open. The roof is protection from the monsoon; for the rest of the year it is an illusion or a useless decoration.*

But then my first impression was followed by another more precise one. One has only to visit the Palace of the Sultan, the Kraton, *to realize that the entire city is a tapestry of alleyways and little houses gathered around the true center from which radiates the influence of the sovereign. The sultan's palace, a sultan much esteemed because he resisted the Dutch and facilitated the path to*

Indonesian independence, is a big empty space of walls and elegant roofs. But above all, it is a center from which the gigantic compound surrounded by walls radiates out. The city lives within itself, and the fast-flowing streets are accessories to its life. The reasons of the inhabitants are still those of subjects of a more general rationality. It's as if Islam here has become clearly affirmed as the right to a secluded daily routine and defended by a central power which is not invasive but embraces everyone a bit. Jogjakarta is an autonomous region and the sultan still exercises a conspicuous power—symbolic above all—over the lives of the citizens. The Kraton, his palace, is closely linked to the volcano Madiri and to the sea. Every New Year the sultan "weds" the Queen of the Southern Sea, the goddess of the Indian Ocean, in whose honor copious gifts are brought to the palace. This opening up of political space to such strong surroundings is the key that centers Jogjakarta and motivates its citizens, much more so than the disintegration of the urban structure brought on by modernization. But the matrix is still visible, and the way of interior living has the villa with the roof like a witch's hat as its ideal model, which has coupled the colonial spirit with tropical intelligence, all glass, verandas, white and green woodwork, and magnificent and triumphant vegetation.

When I rode away on my motorbike toward Borobudur, I saw in my mind's eye the description given by Clifford Geertz of the irrigation system in Java. The countryside is as startling as the city, neat and orderly, its waterways, whether channeled into canals or running free in the rivers, flow through walls and banks that are scrupulously clean, with nary a plastic bag to be seen. One sees how the regime of the waters reflects the regime of the ruler, which allows four harvests each year and discreet wealth for the local agriculturalists. Along the way are beautiful, simple houses with tiled roofs always in the shape of the witch's hat. These are lined along the banks of the canals and serve as a small bridge to the highway filled with mopeds, cars, and the occasional bike. These are houses that speak of rural well-being, a modest pride, and a relationship between rice-paddies and fields, a habitat that is an old, old story.

NOTES

1   Walter Benjamin, *Critiche e recensioni: Tra avanguardie e letteratura di consumo* (Turin: Einaudi, 1979).

2   Franco La Cecla, *Good Morning Karaoke* (Milan: TEA, 2004).

3   Tim Ingold, *Making: Anthropology, Archaeology, Art and Architecture* (London: Routledge, 2013).

4   Lewis Mumford, *The Culture of Cities* (New York: Harcourt, Brace, 1938).

5   Franco La Cecla, *Jet-Lag* (Turin: Bollati Boringhieri, 2002).

6   Riccardo Arena, *La letteratura tamil a Napoli* (Milan: Neri Pozza, 2014).

CHAPTER 3

Why Did Urban Planning Go So Wrong?

WHY HAS URBAN PLANNING TURNED OUT SO BADLY? Today the cities' authority is the most shocking expression of our general schizophrenia. Cities have become the places where one increases or runs though one's wealth, the repository in which one stashes away the hopes of a link with the rest of the world and at the same time they are the places in which one would like to live better. They are invested with the word *globalization*, and those who live there get used to looking at their own city from outside, as part of something that "should happen" or "is happening elsewhere." And so it is that we end up being led by the financial guru and the ideology of homogenization. Nevertheless, we are unable to lose the notion of living exactly here and not somewhere else.[1]

One plays out the destiny of globalization in cities, because is it from this starting point that one submits to its effects or resists them. The problem is that this bipolarity in which all of us who live in cities are enmeshed is a schizophrenia of the cities themselves. Places like Kuala Lumpur want to become world-class cities according to the dictates of a different elsewhere that has nothing to do with the real and daily lives of the people who live there. One might say the same thing about Barcelona's transformation of itself into a brand, where the logistics of normal everyday living have been sacrificed, along with the convivial and close-knit tapestry which used to characterize it, in order to enrich itself with an image as a city of the young and of tourism, which has absolutely nothing to do with the "internal" identity of the city itself. And today Barcelona is paying the price of this total alienation.[2] The point is that cities have both things: an internal side, with the identity of belonging, and an external one, representing a wider scale, and the image imposed from outside. The urban planner has conquered the external side and has mislaid the capacity for reading the internal side.

Today this discipline is afflicted with a poverty laden down with slogans and views seen from drones or helicopters. No one represents this intellectual poverty in which urban planners find themselves better than Rem Koolhaas. His grasshopper vision jumps in a cosmopolitan way from one city to another, Rotterdam, Dubai, Venice, Singapore, New York, Lagos, to make us believe that at the end of the day cities are all reducible to the same parameters.[3] Koolhaas, like every cynic, is a conservative, and in this homogenizing judgment there is a sense of fatalism that is a little reactionary: it's as if he wants to tell us that it is better to abandon all illusions, cities are all capital cities, whether they are real or symbolic, they are caught in the jaws of George Soros or Guy Debord: financial city or show city.

The problem is that he is myopic, both with us and with urban planning, myopic regarding the experience of those who live in cities, myopic regarding the real way of life of city-dwellers. He sees the sense of urban belonging in a radically different way. To understand what cities are internally, it is necessary to reverse the paradigm, to be able to see what, deafened by the sound of globalization claiming to be the singular reality, we have lost from view.

Obviously the rest also exists, the image of themselves that cities want to present, and then there is the way in which some cities make their fortune by relying on their external aspect, Dubai most of all. A city which exists as a hub of popular demands, for all comers, constitutes a new worldliness of power and money. Dubai is the Cannes of today, and almost unthinkable things happen there, deriving from the fact that a good number of politicians from countries such as India are spending time there, making major decisions there, switching their careers, becoming engaged to starlets, shipwrecking their fortunes. It is a tacky Cannes dedicated to the worst in glamour architecture that the archistar system can provide, but which will serve the emir by saving his country when the oil runs out.

Often those who read cities like Dubai do it with the same moralism which in Koolhaas is called cynicism and in Mike Davis, Marxism,[4] that is, the idea that we are faced with something that is "the way the world of money works" and we stop there, without reading all the implications and the forms of resistance to the implications. Even in their best theories, urban theorists of today, from David Harvey[5] to Mike Davis, are afflicted with materialistic fatalism, the same thing that the dandy Rem Koolhaas does so well and makes him acquire in our eyes the patina of Petronius Arbiter. Materialistic fatalism gives the headiness of having the same weapons of capital, of the great market, of globalization; in actuality these complex realities are always far more advanced in materialism than the competing dandies or Marxists or neo-Marxists could ever be. Dialectical materialism is today the self-regulating excuse mechanism of informed capital. Their reasons appear to be those of sound realism.

In order to stand up to it, one has to believe not in the power of the material, but in the power of the spirit, the power of the collective drift of dreams, the strength of the dialectic of meaning that people attach to their own daily lives in spite of everything.

The schizophrenic situation in which we find ourselves is well-illustrated in the account by Alan Hudson regarding Shanghai, which during the 2010 Expo was proposed as the new world city, a city launched by the unprecedented new Chinese economy. The construction of the Expo site required the displacement of the inhabitants living there, a partial transfer

because only a segment of them were assigned housing elsewhere. Alan Hudson went to interview them in their new placement, in the Pudong area, a forty-five-minute metro ride from
the site of the Expo and discovered that the major part of the
resettled people considered their situation to be uncomfortable,
above all because they missed the close ties to their old neighborhood. Moreover, the increased distance from the center of
the city made it much more difficult to sustain the great part of
the activities they had carried out before. But the most exem-
plary situation was the campaign launched by the municipality
of Shanghai against the custom, typical of the inhabitants, of
going to the shopping mall or the market wearing pajamas. The
campaign was carried out by young volunteers who shouted:
"Auntie, do you think it makes our city look good to see you in
your pajamas?" Actually, pajamas are a status symbol of the idea
of comfort and the fact itself of being able to be seen wearing
them: the completely intimate idea of living in a place where
one could move around as if one were in one's own home. But
of course, as far as the occidental tourists coming to Shanghai
were concerned, the custom of auntie in her pajamas would be
counterproductive.

> The urban planner often works on a grand scale, while
> the inhabitant and potential city-dweller looks at the
> world from a more particular point of view. There are
> various places where these two points of view can inter-
> sect. The archetype is the park, or the shopping center
> or the theater, or an institution like a health center or a
> council office. In Shanghai there is a continuous back-
> and-forth between the global and the local, but much
> less between the urban planner who works for the gov-
> ernment and the person who is living in the city. The
> planner offers an anemic version of what he believes
> will be the vision of the international visitor—the turgid
> bar in the Xintiandi district, "the living-room of the

city," superimposed on the antique and characteristic
architecture of the *shikumen*, houses surrounding a large
courtyard—while the city is changing all around him.[6]

Another example of schizophrenia is the struggle in
Shanghai, as well as in other cities in China, to defend the right
to hang clothes out to dry in the open air. The national and
local governments are not in agreement. Drying laundry is not
a sight for tourists, giving the idea that China is a backward
country (and full of bumpkins). The inhabitants don't agree,
insisting on invading parking spaces and courtyards, light poles
and any other support, to hang out their own clothes, as well
as constructing architectural spaces for spreading out laundry
that changes the appearance of the skyscrapers. The right to
dry clothes in the fresh air (because, they say, this is a humid
country and they won't get dry indoors) extends even to the
fiftieth-floor occupants of a popular skyscraper. Iron constructions, with tubes twenty-meters or longer, sprout from the
windows like so many fishing poles, like so many quadrilaterals
from which nets are suspended, and the clothes fish the sky for
favorable drying winds.[7]

Fukuoka, Japan
*Like every Japanese city, this one resembles a toy construction kit.
The houses, the apartment buildings, the streets, the sidewalks, seem
to be part of a scale model, not like the ones you find in an architect's
studio, more like Lego bricks or something that betrays a kind of
immateriality, as if the city didn't want to possess any kind of severity. For sure it is an aspect of postwar logistics. Japan, in order to
make people forget, and to forget about the war, had to remove the
most frightening aspect from their own urban aesthetic, that of a
severity which couples precision and the cult of nationalistic values.
The postwar era saw frantic reconstruction, dominated by a need to
cancel out the past. From this comes the rationale of the cute, the
pretty, which pervades the buildings, streets, and urban furnishings*

and which seems to make everything conform with the essence of anime and manga. This works well for the builders, but less so for the inhabitants. The Japanese have maintained a domestic urban dimension that still prevails in even the most trafficked and central areas. Behind the skyscrapers and the motorways, there is a constant network of roji, of little streets that run parallel to the main streets and onto which the doorways of private houses face. Sometimes these roji, which fill a role similar to that of English mews, are paved in a different way from the main streets and sometimes they are not even paved. Along them one can move around in yukata dressing gown and slippers or, better yet, in dressing gown and flip-flops.

Fukuoka nevertheless is possessed of modern architecture and urban furnishings and equipped with public/private microspaces. Being a place of the "south," some of the characteristics of its street-life are very distinctive. For example, here one can eat on the street in special little huts called yatai. Mounted on wheels, and curtained off, they can become real and true restaurants installed right on the sidewalk. There are about two hundred of them, the majority in Tenjin and Nakasu. Besides tonkatsu ramen, a local soup, they also serve yakiniku, horumon, and tempura. The characteristic of these places is that they appear in the evening, vanish into the night, and then reappear the following evening. They cluster together in middle-class and upper-middle-class districts and everyone considers them the best places to eat. Every evening each of these little huts has its group of young people who regularly gather there, but there are people of all ages who eat and, above all, drink sake, but also shochu (really strong alcohol made from potatoes or barley). The contrast between the surrounding buildings and the little huts is striking, as if in an orderly and distinctly middle-class city of apartment buildings made of concrete and glass there suddenly appeared temporary constructions of tin and tar paper. This sidelight characterizes the popular view of the city and its base of mixing Korean traditions (Korea is very close by) with those of southern Japan.

If on the other hand you make your way to the island, which is in the midst of the river and constitutes a kind of city center, you'll become aware of another very common characteristic of Japanese urban life: that of setting the red-light district apart. The entertainment district here, as in many other Japanese cities, is a kind of stronghold of bars, of lounge-bars, of karaoke bars, and of restaurants and cafes designed to attract those in search of feminine company. The central section of Fukuoka offers a well-defined choice in this matter. In front of each business there is a list of the women from which one may select one's own companion. It is not a question of simple prostitution, but of every possible shade of entertainment. One may go from drinking a beer with a student who is looking to make ends meet, to the most professional of escorts, to every subtle gradation of sexual fulfillment.

The striking thing is that this is a characteristic that stamps the urban conformation of a good part of Japanese cities in such a way that it is only occidental visitors who comment on it. The fact that a sizable chunk of the city is devoted to the red-light district seems to remain buried in the subconscious of its inhabitants. It forms a part of the same landscape as the shopping malls and the offerings of the restaurants and the snack shacks. It's a city that refuses entry to those who are not expert consumers. Thus, westerners are unable to enter easily into this world and are unable to understand its rules. Physically, being "apart" manifests itself through the lights and illuminated signs which invite entry to those who are not open to any of the scenarios, in the sense that being outside they are unable to understand what is happening inside, precisely because the rationality is that of a totally Japanese "privateness" offered as companionship. They hear the music from below, they glimpse the glow of the lights, and sometimes, very rarely, they will even run across women in the streets who offer themselves as entertainers inside.

What does this type of urban organization have to offer for those who live there? How does it inform the day or the week? What do the women who don't work there have to say about it and what does it give rise to in the male population? And above all, what do those who live there have to say about the "secretiveness" that this type of organization has to say to strangers about them? The

*red-light island is the nighttime city as opposed to the daytime one;
it's a part of what one does after work, of the time when one goes out
with colleagues to eat and drink and be in the company of women.
I wonder if at least a part of the male and female population lives a
little uneasily with the fact that the amusement sector is so spread
out and such an integrated part of the urban landscape. Is it seen as
a resource, like a relief after the work of the day, as a distraction on
a par with what we think of as the evening and nighttime downtown
in one of our own cities? Is it invisible during the day?*

NOTES

1   Jonathan Friedman, *La quotidianità del sistema globale*, eds. Franco La Cecla
    and Piero Zanini (Milan: Bruno Mondadori, 2008); Franco La Cecla and
    Piero Zanini, *Una morale per la vita di tutti i giorni* (Milan: Eleuthera, 2012).

2   Franco La Cecla, *Against Architecture* (Oakland: PM Press/The Green
    Arcade, 2012).

3   Rem Koolhaas, *Junkspace: Per un ripensamento radicale dello spazio urbano*
    (Rome: Quodlibet, 2006).

4   Mike Davis, "Fear and Money in Dubai," *New Left Review*, no. 41 (2006):
    47–68.

5   David Harvey, *The Urban Experience* (Baltimore: Johns Hopkins University
    Press, 1989); Harvey, *Seventeen Contradictions and the End of Capitalism*
    (Oxford: Oxford University Press, 2014).

6   Alan Hudson, "The Dynamic City: Citizens Make Cities," in *The Lure of
    the City: From Slums to Suburbs*, eds. Austin Williams and Alastair Donald
    (London: Pluto Press, 2011), 29.

7   Anna Laura Govoni, http://www.pinterest.com/gaoal/.

CHAPTER 4

Why Urban Planning Doesn't Help Us Understand Cities

THE REAL PROBLEM WITH URBAN PLANNING IS THAT IT is unable to put itself together as a discipline concerned with observing, hearing and interpreting urban reality. The complexity of city living seems to interest urban planners only minimally, accustomed as they are to chase after more or less drastic solutions tied to an application that has scarcely changed in the past fifty years. The not-very-edifying spectacle of the plans presented for the "Grand Paris" is a profound testimony to this.[1] The representation of the spectrum is still just an "atlas" made up of networks, flows, and zoning plans in which it is extremely difficult to recognize not only a *genius loci*, but above all a connecting affiliation and mutual influence between the inhabitants and the city. It seems as if the city were made up once and for all, from definite forces, financial dealers or speculators, administrations, companies, traffic management, as well as ecology and sustainability. Even the new word "sustainability"—well, a few decades old now—has predictably remade itself to define totally different needs. To which needs is sustainability the key? It should mean making use of resources in such a manner that they will be there for future generations to enjoy. Now, as Unni Wikan teaches us in her review of the evaluation criteria of "sustainability" for a city such as Cairo, nothing is said in the experts' plans about an effective improvement for the poor of the city.[2] The poor of Cairo among whom she has worked for

forty years have effectively improved their own lives by means
of their network of solidarity which they have strengthened
for themselves in the absence of public interventions: mar-
riages remain solid, crime is low, the children go to school, and,
once they are grown up, they are able, by means of informal
self-sufficiency, to acquire an apartment where the new couple
can live in the center, away from the quarter. The point is that a
good part of this life slips by city planning because the question
of understanding is never put in place as a discipline. Unlike
other disciplines that deal with social life, it persists in remaining an area where it falls prey to the statistical projections of the
experts. Who sets the hierarchical priority? What comes first for
the inhabitants of a city? The right to a roof over one's head or
the right to a life dependent on relationships of solidarity? The
right to consume or the right to produce goods? The right to
health or the right of access to resources that render health possible: wells, springs, and the possibility of managing the disposal
of dirty water and garbage?

Yet it all started under the best auspices. Among the
founding fathers of urban planning was a Russian prince who
had embraced the cause of the Revolution, but with a viewpoint
that separated itself from materialism and the Bolshevik violence
and instead went to the roots of the community history of the *mir*,
the advisors of the rural villages in Russia.[3] Kropotkin had spent
his youth exploring the geography of the huge northern part of
Russia and had refined the measurements and mapping of the
area without ever losing sight of the human aspect, the animist
and shamanic aspect of the Siberian culture that he encountered
there. And in the midst of the reindeer breeders he found
throughout that vast icy region he discovered what he called
"mutual aid," the reciprocity of the nomad communities.[4] When
he was expelled from Russia for his revolutionary activities, he
found himself traveling around the world and developing a new
geography which slowly translated itself into an idea of city and
of territory linked to the human output of social cohesion and

the management of space. True urban planning was born when Patrick Geddes was inspired by Kropotkin to develop the tools for studying cities and possible intervention practices.[5] Also a great traveler, he divided his time between India and his native Scotland, as he put together the base of a humanistic matrix for development and urban planning.

This thread was taken up by another great scholar, Lewis Mumford, who put his seal of approval on the approach with his magnificent fresco of the "culture of cities." Mumford was inspired by the same matrix of geographic anarchism as Kropotkin.[6] Cities are, first and foremost, the place where human cohabitation happens, and they have to be regarded as such; cities are nothing else but people, as Shakespeare's famous line recalls: "What is the city but the people?" From Kropotkin to Mumford there is a channel of testimony which opens up the most specific geography of cities and, in Mumford's case, links this approach to the observation of American cities, an extraordinary case of cohabitation on a grand scale which erupted into history like a novelty that basically reappraises all of human existence. It is not by chance that Mumford talks of the "culture of cities," an approach that gets away from an idea of planning from on high and instead identifies the making of cities as one of the most ancient characteristics of human endeavor.

Arriving at the fifties, perhaps it was actually then that this incredibly rich approach came up against a totally technical idea of urban planning; perhaps it's precisely what happened in New York, when we see Jane Jacobs, author of *The Death and Life of Great American Cities* (1961), militating against Robert Moses, the "principal planner" who would saw off the Bronx from the rest of the city with the construction of the Cross Bronx Expressway and the imposition of a zoning plan on the democratic New York grid which would facilitate the separation of social classes and diverse ethnicities.[7] The New York "Moses Plan" can be compared to a capital project where one wants to construct a city based on land revenue, leading to the expulsion of the heterogeneity that up until now made up the composition of the city. Jacobs fought all her life against this type of structuring, and she did it alternating her pursuit of knowledge and town planning with organizing local protest groups.

So what happens after? All over the world the idea emanates that city planning is a "technique" in the hands of some experts, who, with an almost divine intuition, "see" the city from on high and "redesign" it. The "artistic vein" is concentrated in the hands of the urban planners, who in the early times of international architecture would seem destined to compete with the architects, the "artists of the city." Already in the 1933 Athens Charter of CIAM (Congrès Internationaux d'Architecture Moderne), this aspect was making itself evident. Architects are also in part city planners because they share with them the "flash of genius" that makes it possible to see things on a grand scale without knowing the formal view of urban planning itself. At the end of the day the urban planning forms correspond with the architectural plans, volumes, and surfaces, and in either case it's a question of intervening with taste and a formal competence which is possessed only by those who are formed by the art of design. And it is at this point that urban planning loses its attention to human actions, to the lived experience and above all to making the city into a prime location to be relished by those who live in it. From Bauhaus to the international architecture of Le Corbusier it is all a reference to the "sense of proportion" which is inherent in an aesthetic discipline. The point is that any problem is minimized by the change of scale. It is as if in architecture the necessary aptitude for managing forms could be immediately transferred to the urban context. Anyone who wishes to follow this transformation could use a valuable resource such as the *Chronology of the Urban Thought*, (*Cronologia do Pensamento Urbanistico*) put together by the Laboratório de Estudos Urbanos (LeU) Cultura Urbana e Pensamento Urbanístico.[8] The chronology is constructed so as to give the scenario of the evolution (or of the involution) of city planning on various continents, faithful to the credo of the Modern Movement for Architecture and the tenets of CIAM.

From the viewpoint of scientific development, it is here that urban planning as a discipline loses whatever pretext it may have had of "knowing" the city and is no longer instrumental to it. (Let's leave this waste of time to the theorists—Kevin Lynch, Reyner Banham, Roberti Venturi—while they busy themselves with the construction of new world capitals like Chandigarh or Brasilia or Le Corbusier utopias—such as razing Paris to the ground with the Plan Voisin. It was not by chance that Le Corbusier made this proposition in 1925 and then a little before the Second World War offered it again as a proposition for reconstruction of the city in case of a bombardment.) Instead of knowing this, urban planning maintains that it advances its own aesthetic utopias, as if urban phenomenology were made up solely of structures, and that the bonds and networks and imperceptible purposes of those who live there and those who come to live there are completely unimportant. Urban planning becomes the handmaiden of architectural formalism and easily sells itself to those who call on it solely to ratify the biggest deci-sions: the huge land speculations that started in the fifties in all the European and American cities and, in opposition to them, the state-run "development" that surfaced in the East, where the state conducted itself like a true real-estate holding, and was then imitated in Europe, beginning in France with enormous projects like the Grands Ensembles.[9]

Urban planning "a la Mumford" would actually have a revival in England in the sixties and seventies, starting out from Ebenezer Howard's idea of a "garden city" that would inspire a reflux of the New Towns movement. The construction of these satellite cities would reprise of the debate between liberal origins and anarchy and a search for the development of community models for the new settlements. In Italy it would be Carlo Doglio, tireless mentor of Anglo-Saxon culture of libertarian origins in the postwar Italian world, with stiff Catholic/Marxist opposition.[10] Doglio would translate Mumford, Peter Kropotkin, Patrick Geddes, and Jayprakash Narayan, the great Indian politician who drew on libertarian ideas from Geddes.[11] Moreover, Doglio would take part in the world of Olivetti's experimental communities in Ivrea and later in Danilo Dolci's nonviolent experiments and social activism from the ground up. Doglio himself would develop a "social activism from below" theory that would influence people close to him like Giancarlo De Carlo and also influence urban planning on a regional scale, which would be put into practice in the seventies in Emilia-Romagna.

One might wonder what happened and how this whole thing came to be so forgotten today. What could have happened to make Henri Lefebvre say in his *The Right to the City* (1968) that the problem is that urban planning has done away with city life. For Lefebvre city life means the productive activity that people do normally in the city by living there. For the scholarly Frenchman in the seventies, it was already a question of recovering a visibility that was being lost. The urban planning of the planning department, the urban planning assigned for private study, the urban planning understood as the "handling" of the relative question of "who has the right to build and where" departs entirely from its humanistic matrix and completely loses sight of the need for giving itself the resources of the knowledge which should be guiding its participation.

More than forty years have passed since then, and by now the idea of the urban planner as a "quantum" technician, an expert in trends, a kind of assistant in the real estate economy, a political go-between able to mediate among the forces of territorial capital, is so successful that it seems obvious. But the devastating effects are before the eyes of everyone. When it comes to the disasters caused by architects, city planners are able to take cover in a veil of semi-invisibility. They have no interest in becoming superstars in the glossy magazines or at the Venice Biennale.

Glamour doesn't beckon them, because they are inter-
ested in the *real stuff*, that is, they are interested in transforming
urban territory into economy on a grand scale. Urban planning
becomes something that can be quoted on the stock market,
played in the same way as derivatives or futures projections,
and planners can woo politicians with the idea that this has
need of a "governance" that only the experts can offer. Today
urban planners place themselves in the ambiguous but very
remunerative area of political administrative weakness and the
shortsightedness of speculative finance. They offer politicians
the reassurance that they can devote themselves to their own
images and not have to worry about running the city, and to
financiers they present the idea of long-projected incomes over
wild speculation.

How does it happen that a story that starts out so well
finishes up so badly?

Skipping over several years, there is today a revival of the
idea of "garden cities" through New Urbanism, founded in
California, and represented especially by Peter Calthorpe.[12] But
it is not by chance that one of Peter Calthorpe's most brilliant
achievements became the scenario for the film *The Truman Show*,
precisely because inside the garden city project the concept of
a separate and protected space is already present. Calthorpe is
currently working in China to spread a new urban-humanistic
paradigm. This "avant-garde" is part of the general debate on city
planning today. For sure he draws criticism in proclaiming to
be the New Urbanism, but many of his tools are those of traditional urban planning. Calthorpe originates from the ecological
and radical thinking of the eighties in California, but he is still
fully into an idea of "an architectural studio." His own quite
large studio is a private company which seeks private and public
clients. A radical criticism of current urban planning would defi-
nitely involve a complete revision of how urban design studios
actually function: they have yet to liberate themselves from the
close similarity they have to the studios of the archistars.

Meanwhile there has been a renewal in architecture. The figure of the architect and the role of architects in society have been put in a difficult position, so they are searching for new paths. Among the first: the redefining of the rapport between the client and the job. If architects are to transform the direction and the destination of their work, then it is essential for them to be the one selecting the commission, favoring the social commission, the one that has the most need of his competence— from the inhabitants of the *favelas* (shantytowns) to community subjects to indigent populations in states of emergency: earthquakes, floods, manmade and natural disasters. From the nineties on in various parts of the world, the idea was born that professional studios would be able to turn themselves into true and real nongovernmental organizations who could work around "social questions." In order to do this, some groups of professionals joined together using the resources offered today by the internet and assembled studios that on the one hand identify "where to operate" in rapport with these communities and on the other hand seek funds and sponsors for their own work. Architecture is a bit of a latecomer in discovering the world of contemporary "philanthropy" and in inserting itself into the grand strand of nongovernmental organizations with their issues of independence or not from the sponsors. The most organized and best-trained group today is Architecture for Humanity,[13] founded a dozen or so years ago by Cameron Sinclair, a young English architect relocated to California. They have brilliantly made available their charismatic capacities for attracting to their project the attention of big foundations such as the Clinton Foundation, the Google Foundation, Benetton, Enel Cuore, and the Gates Foundation. The genius of AFH is that they have separated the research for funds from the research on the situations in which they are intervening and have given a character to their own interventions that pays attention to local contexts. No project happens without local partners, not just communities, villages, and base organizations, but also professionals and local architects. And in order to work with AFH, one has to guarantee to work within the budget and to follow up. The project is overseen from the beginning, and then monitored after it is completed. The formula is working so well that today AFH has eighteen thousand professionals throughout the world who together make a network that also gives up the copyright of their projects (which can be seen in detail on the internet), and they are present in forty-four countries around the world. The most important point is that a good proportion of the professionals are architects who were tired of the type of logic behind the classic architectural studio. The drawback of AFH is that they work in a very "architectural" way, that is on single buildings or groups of dwellings, services, and reconstructions of infrastructures at times, but they do not work with a wider view of the effect on cities. I say "drawback," but it is also one of their merits, that of confining themselves to architectural expertise. Obviously in the field of urban planning this sort of approach has still to happen.

From a theoretical point of view, a certain American New Left that ranged from David Harvey to Mike Davis took up Lefebvre's arguments on the "right to the city."[14] Davis had the merit of having started from a detailed analysis of the districts, specifically the case of Los Angeles in *City of Quartz* and then in successive works dealing with analyzing events or situations in other contexts and times. Davis has also written the first book of full disclosure about slums, an ample and startling denunciation of that phenomenon in *Planet of Slums*.[15] David Harvey goes back to the centrality of the urban question in the neo-Marxist key (whereas Lefebvre relieved himself of this weight). For Harvey, the city would be the real "central" place of capital today, because it is the place where its excessive accumulation occurs. So urban struggles and rebellions would today be central to the fight against capitalism and neoliberalism.[16] While reading both of these, it must be said that at a certain point one wonders if the stubbornness of wanting to offer a general system of reading

that would be consistent with Marxism may create little respon-
siveness from all the human components of cities. Yet in their
analyses it seems that when all is said and done, for the subjects that have undergone the logistics of capital there really
remains very little space to operate whether out of desperation
or because of the unequal struggle. They do not see what James
C. Scott (another distinguished analyst of the current situation, about whom we have already spoken in the first chapter)
instead calls "resistance," the capacity of the individual and communities not only to oppose but to constitute society.[17] Scott's
society is autopoietic; it generates itself like Walter Benjamin's,
between individual or collective initiatives, between the drift-
ing-off of sleepwalkers[18] or the aims of revolutionaries, but
above all, it manifests itself in the production of daily life, that
ability to build bonds and establish settlements with common
motivations, in short, what anthropologists call culture, and
what would be the world, built or not, of relationships between
people and places, the network of reciprocity that supports and
drives a society.[19]

The disciplinary charter of anthropology primarily focuses
attention on society "making itself." It is not by chance that
Marshall Sahlins, one of the great anthropologists of our time,
criticizes Foucault and his "structuralist" outline precisely
because it allows society almost no autonomy. Born from
Marxism but prolonged by its structuralist currents, this is a
failure to perceive not only individual but also collective subjectivity.[20] Individuals and even groups would be buffeted by supe-
rior opposing forces and above all immersed for a good part in
illusions created by those in power, whether these be ideologies
or shopping or show business. As Agamben notes in a recent
article on Guy Debord,[21] private space is itself enhanced in
order to then to be crushed and denied. One could take refuge
in privacy if this effectively saves us from the force fields that
influence our life, but in the long run it seems that private life is
only a kind of clandestine intimacy even in its most irreverent

forms and boundary-pushing practices (from sadomasochism to orgiastic friendships).

Anthropology, observing the phenomenology of communities, has something quite different to say. Not only can individuals always present themselves as exceptions, but human groups are "acting" and making communities even when they don't know it. Daily life is a way of producing community, something that elsewhere, together with Piero Zanini, I have called the production of "a precept for everyday life"—the routines, the daily rhythms, the collective dreams. These currents create spaces within which everyday nature develops its autonomy from external force-fields and becomes a force-field itself. In Indonesia, for example, recently, at a request for the application of Sharia law, the facts proved that it is the *adat*, the system of habits and usages and correct behavior, which is much more important as the basis of the law. The customary right based on correct behavior in public prevailed over an outside imposition.

Anthropology has much to teach urban planning, in this sense. The production of community, of "the way of life," of relationships among people make the city much more than a bunch of real estate or of some planning strategy. If it does not learn to comprehend this type of production (conscious or unconscious), urban planning is ready to be thrown away.

Istanbul, Turkey

Istanbul, Constantinople, Byzantium—no city is more evocative than this one. And as with all true cities it's difficult to embrace it with one look, difficult to have a concise idea of it. It is one of those places that is elusive and fascinating at the same time. The eyes get tired faced with the incredible richness of the views, of the glimpses, the details. One gets a physical longing to conquer it, to get to know every detail, to be able to live in its twists and turns and to have points of reference within them. For me in the last three years it has become a kind of obsession. I arrived there and realized, as I do every time, that I'm inadequate. It folded me into its complexity, I remained totally impressed as much by its beauty as by the ugliness of its immense surroundings, I was bewitched by the impossible tilt of Beyoğlu as well as by the interminable extension of the Asian quarters. I fell asleep in the taxi taking me to Sabiha Gokcen Airport and reawoke to find myself surrounded by neighborhoods and minarets of the worst workmanship, but then around a curve there appeared the Sea of Marmara, the Principi Islands, a string of waiting navy ships. Istanbul is a city of twenty-three million inhabitants, a dimension to which we Europeans are unaccustomed. In this sense it is Asian on a par with Beijing, Jakarta, Mumbai. But at the same time, it is incredibly Roman, it is the second Rome, and one can still feel that. This is the capital of an empire. When you get there you just have time to drop off your luggage before you start exploring, and every time it is different. You start out from the places accessible to tourists, Istiklâl Caddesi, the elegant broad and European street which is the axis that leads to Beyoğlu, that is, to the old Greek and Genoese quarter of Pera and Galata. And already it seems complicated because you can't understand how people are able to live on such dizzying levels of steepness constructed on the sheer and overbuilt hill over the Bosporus. And your explorations take you to the bottom of the valley where the gypsies live, in gullies full of shacks, unthinkable that it's a couple of steps away from Orhan Pamuk's Museum of Innocence, then wearily you surmount other slopes until you find yourself in the oasis of Cihangir, where you sit in a peaceful cafe and drink a chai, and in front of you there is a little mosque, and next to it arbors and below more little cafes. It is a city marked by tiring climbs and unexpected relaxing spots. In every corner you will see stools and little tables outside shops and homes. You want to sit down, but you can't, because these are not public spaces but an extension of private spaces into the street. Unless you are invited to do so. Already you're a victim of the first spell. Because between the tiring climbs and the steep descents unthinkable patches open up, ferries that seem to snuggle between the edge of a house and the framework of a mosque, slivers of the sparkling Bosporus that open up at the end of a series of stairways. It is a clambering, clinging and very downmarket city, constructed according to necessity and not according to plans, using minimal spaces that appear to be monumental at the same time. A web in Beyoğlu resembles the alleyways of Genoa or the lanes in Barcelona, but which however has a kind of centuries-old major temporariness, between the abandoned ruins, and the climbing plants which have taken over. Here you realize that only if you go on foot, step by step, can you get an idea of it. And if you do it, you will find yourself following the Istanbulis and their own very particular way of life. So, scrambling headlong down from Cihangir you find yourself in Tophane, in front of the Bosporus and finishing up at Kabataş to wait around like everyone for the ferry to continue on, into Asia, to Scutari, as it was known when this was Constaninople and which nowadays is known as Üsküdar. The normality of this densely constructed city is magnificent with its mirrors of water to be crossed. They are the breaks that the commuters give themselves, here on the wooden ferries already familiar in the twentieth century and where there is also time for a chai, a tea in the bell-shaped glasses that one learns to hold at the top so as not to burn one's fingers, like the Istanbulis, with the thumb and index finger supporting the rim. The Bosporus astounds with its grandeur and for at the same time being so close, with the anglers rounding out supper with their rods and lines, while at the same time the waters are filled with cargo ships from afar, from the Black Sea and the great Greek Archipelago, from Egypt and Crimea. Arriving on the other side you start again to conquer on foot another piece of the mystery. And here in Üsküdar, in the Asian quarter, you realize that this city is much more complex than its contemporary description. In Kuzguncuk, a suburb of Üsküdar, you are astonished to count Armenian and Orthodox churches, and side by side the walls of synagogues and mosques. You are surprised that the multiethnic and multireligious past are so present. And only as you make your way through it, do you discover how much this city is filled with Armenian and Orthodox cemeteries and how much the imprint of the Greeks is still so very alive. Not only in the sacred places, but also in the profane ones. The mehane, the little restaurants that front on the

Bosporus, are the Greek tavernas where one used to drink, and one still drinks (in spite of the government's attempts to limit alcohol) that anise distillation which is called arak and which quenches the thirst of a good slice of the eastern Mediterranean. The great producers were Greek, and it was only in the sixties that they had to leave. Today for the young people of Gezi Park wanting to revive an endangered secular lifestyle, that past is slowly beginning to reemerge. Istanbul is a crossroads of cultures and religions, it is the bridge between East and West and today it is the hope of a dialogue between Europe and the Near East. It is difficult not to be moved when after five or six times you have come here to explore and you realize that it is the evidence of the city you have conquered with your feet that tells you its history, much better than any guide. Turning back to Beyoğlu you return to the upper-class quarter, Nişantşi, the place where for the most part the protagonists in Pamuk's novels live, and there you make another discovery. To begin with, this apparently more modern part is scarred by the same precipices and cliffs as the old part. At such a point the Istanbulis discovered a system of funiculars which serve as shortcuts. And then down among the tall palaces of the fine folks, beyond the Pradas and the Guccis, you find yourself again in a popular neighborhood, where skewers of lamb are sizzling, in Şişli, side by side with the immense Armenian cemetery. Here too you are walking on ridges looking out on the Bosporus, you stop in front of wagons with grapes and garbanzos, you are amazed at the variety of food brought in on carts and offered to passersby like you. You sit down and take your ease on a bench shaded by flourishing vines as you find yourself in a little alley where the city has given way to the country. All this makes you realize that you are not dealing with a city but with a universe and that the memories represented by the monuments, stones, rocks, and inscriptions are not a dive into the past but a hypothesis of the future, the experience of a rich world where diverse affiliations become written off from common rootedness in a place unique in the world. The nostalgia of those who have to leave it, Christian, Jew, Sufi, or Armenian, is transformed into a solid feeling. At times it has given birth to a genre of music such as the rebetiko, a Greek style of music played on stringed instruments that is similar to Balkan jazz and has the same aching nostalgia. But the same thing has happened with other types of music, like the fazil, the music of the local people, where they played a kind of oriental strain that came to be called arabesque and which was then forbidden for years because it was not Turkish enough. Today we are at a precious moment when all this richness is reemerging, and it is the young people who are adopting it as their patrimony. And the city is still the strongest evidence of a world capital that is the patrimony of all of Europe and from which Europe has much to learn.

NOTES

1   Augustin Berque, Alessia de Biase, and Philippe Bonnin, eds., *Donner lieu au monde: la poétique de l'habiter: Actes du colloque de Cerisy-la-Salle* (Paris: Donner lieu, 2012). Alessia de Biase is the specialist in charge of the research project "Qualifier la transformation: ou comment se projette l'idee de qualité de vie dans le futur Grand Paris," Projet Urban D–FEDER/Union Europeenne 2010–12.

2   Unni Wikan, *Tomorrow, God Willing: Self-made Destinies in Cairo* (Chicago: University of Chicago Press, 1996).

3   Alexander V. Chayanov, *The Theory of Peasant Economy* (Madison: University of Wisconsin Press, 1986); originally published in Russian in 1925. The 1986 English edition also contains Chayanov's *On the Theory of Non-Capitalist Economic Systems.*

4   Peter A. Kropotkin, *Mutual Aid: A Factor of Evolution* (London: Heinemann, 1902; repr. London: Freedom Press, 1998).

5   Patrick Geddes, *Utopian Papers: Being Addresses to "The Utopians"* (London: Masters, 1908); Geddes, *Cities in Evolution: An Introduction to the Town Planning Movement and to the Study of Civics* (London: Williams and Norgate, 1915).

6   Lewis Mumford, *The Culture of Cities* (New York: Harcourt, Brace, 1938); *The City in History* (New York: Harcourt, Brace, 1961); *The Story of Utopias* (New York: Boni and Liveright, 1922).

7   Marshall Berman, *All That Is Solid Melts into Air* (New York: Penguin, 1982).

8   Cronologia do Pensamento Urbanístico, http://www.cronologiadourbanismo.ufba.br/.

9   Franco La Cecla, *Against Architecture* (Oakland: PM Press/The Green Arcade, 2012).

10   Carlo Doglio, *La città giardino: Crisi dell'utopia, città e urbanistica di fronte alla rivoluzione industriale* (Rome: Gangemi, 1985).

11   Giovanni Ferraro, *Rieducazione alla speranza: Patrick Geddes, planner in India* (Milano: Jaca Book, 1998).

12   Sim Van der Ryn and Peter Calthorpe, *Sustainable Communities: A New Design Synthesis for Cities, Suburbs and Towns* (San Francisco: Sierra Club Books, 1986); Calthorpe, *Urbanism in the Age of Climate Change* (Washington, DC: Island Press, 2010).

13   Now known as Open Architecture Collaborative: http://openarchcollab.org/.

14   Henri Lefebvre, "The Right to the City," in *Writings on Cities*, trans. Eleonore Kofman and Elizabeth Lebas (Oxford: Blackwell, 1996), 63–181; originally published as *Le droit à la ville* (Paris: Anthropos, 1968).

15   Mike Davis, *City of Quartz: Excavating the Future in Los Angeles* (New York: Verso, 1990); Davis, *Planet of Slums* (New York: Verso, 2006).

16   David Harvey, *Rebel Cities: From the Right to the City to the Urban Revolution* (New York: Verso, 2012).

17   James C. Scott, *Domination and the Art of Resistance: Hidden Transcripts* (New Haven, CT: Yale University Press, 1990).

18   Gabriel Tarde, *Che cos'è una società?*, ed. Andrea Cavalletti (Naples: Cronopio, 2010).

19   Franco La Cecla and Piero Zanini, *Una morale per la vita di tutti i giorni* (Milan: Eleuthera, 2010).

20   Marshall Sahlins, *Waiting for Foucault, Still* (Chicago: Prickly Paradigm Press, 2002).

21   Giorgio Agamben, *The Use of Bodies*, trans. Adam Kotsko (Stanford, CA: Stanford University Press, 2016); originally published as *L'uso dei corpi* (Milan: Neri Pozza, 2014).

CHAPTER 5

Against the Word of UN–Habitat: The World Will Be All Urban

TODAY AN IDEOLOGY OF *BIGNESS* PREVAILS,[1] WHICH SEES expansion as the promise of a world of global cities which would give an effect of "prosperity" to the rest of society. If one reads the reports of the United Nations Human Settlements Programme (UN-Habitat) on African, Asian, or Latin American cities,[2] or even the general reports on urban conditions, *prosperity* is the word one sees most frequently. But if one really digs down it becomes apparent that this is a pious illusion. Absolutely nothing in the effect of gargantuan enlargement of cities results in an improvement in the lives of the inhabitants. Instead what becomes clear is that world poverty is being concentrated in cities. And let it not be said that the poor people in the city are better off than the poor people in the country. It depends on the politics of the International Monetary Fund or the World Bank or on the pretexts of international aid organizations, or it depends on the rape of the land, of the land grab by palm oil multinationals, or of the De Ricas and Del Montes. But in cities conditions of hygiene and overcrowding for the poor and the poverty-stricken are anything but prosperous. This word is well chosen because it speaks of the future and not of the present. It's a promise, not evidence. Reports based on projections for 2050 promise a future of global cities and the urbanization of the planet. Today we are 50 percent there, but it is a world average and it is true that entire continents are not yet urbanized. Asia and Africa, where the rural dimension is still of the utmost importance and in many cases preponderant, are not yet urbanized. But it is obviously a menacing threat.

Behind the idea of urban prosperity is the inability of international organisms to call into question the diminishing of subsistence farming due to the growth of the multinationals. The world is becoming so urbanized that peasants can no longer make a living from their own soil. It's hard to understood why the "trends" observed by UN-Habitat don't lead to corrective policies rather than to hoping for a completely urban world. A dangerous ideology is lurking behind the words *urban prosperity*. It is right up there with those who think that the future will be a network of world cities, as if agriculture and the production of food are not equally essential for prosperity and as if in the countryside it would be impossible to model a culture and a way of life different from that in cities, equally rooted in human history and capable of producing culture and society.

The same idea of global cities clashes with the fact that it is really small and medium-sized cities that are growing, but not everywhere. According to international reports on cities, it would seem that entire countries are now living solely on air or on the trickle-down of the indirect benefits of urban expansion, as if no one is producing anything to eat anymore. In reality, if one travels a bit around the continents, there is, in the face of the devastation provoked by agricultural multinationals, a huge pool of resistant small farmers, rice growers, managers of market gardens, small breeders, agriculturists in the mountains and valleys who are more or less organized to live in the country as if it were the best of systems, not only from the point of view of subsistence, but also as the cultural system to which they belong. It's impossible to think of an inhabitant of Toraja without his rice paddy,[3] just as it is impossible to think of a Peruvian mountain dweller without his fields of potatoes. The problem is that we have an image of subsistence agriculture all tied in with the emergency factor of the NGOs and the international organizations. Many small and medium-sized operations (for example in Indonesia) are made up of families who have a house close to the fields and lined up with other similar houses. This is the "rural" middle class about which we hear very little.

The problem is that the urban planning of international organizations is the slave of statistics, rather than of those strange things that are their projections. It seems that all their learning is tied to how to read trends and percentages and to a blind faith in the calculation of probabilities. It is the only remaining discipline to believe in the logarithmic aspect of social phenomena, the handmaid of those "who know more about it," that is, the prophets of globalization today, like the high priests of development yesterday. It seems that they are unencumbered by doubts of any kind.

We have to acknowledge that the world is moving toward becoming completely urban. If reality is not a value, but a factual datum, then faced by a similar eventuality urban planning could invent policies and plans that go in a totally different direction. It is not the first time, for example, and not by chance, that China today is looking worried about its own urban future and running to repair its overly restrictive policies with regard to the urbanization of its rural world. Certainly it is necessary for the Chinese prosopopoeia of the past few years to take a clear step back with regard to bigness and above all to reverse the stigma that during the past two decades has struck the peasant class, guilty of not making themselves rich and of not being consumers. It is an essential question for China, precisely because the devastation of the environment and the countryside is reaching the point of no return and the giddiness of possessing great world cities like Shanghai, Shenzhen, Beijing, and Hong Kong is not worth the price that has to be paid.

The thing that is so astonishing in the UN-Habitat documents on urbanization is that they are subject to a real and true schizophrenia. On the one hand there is the promise of prosperity linked to the growth of cities, and on the other there is the specter of slums. When we look at the way international organizations have treated slums in the past fifty years, we see an incapacity to judge the pros and cons of urbanization. But let's take a step back. What is hidden in the auspices of Habitat, the United Nations organization concerned with human settlements, that the all-urban future of the world brings us prosperity?

The cover of the UN-Habitat report *State of the World's Cities 2012/2013* carries a bias. A wheel with five spokes carries on its circumference: "Environmental Sustainability, Equity and Social Inclusion, Quality of Life, Infrastructure, and Productivity." At the center of these cardinal virtues is the proposed effect, "*Prosperity.*"

In order to understand what is behind this we have to turn to the debate on global cities launched by Saskia Sassen in the nineties. Sassen, analyzing three great world cities—Tokyo, New York, and London (I would have added Seoul, Shanghai, Beijing, and others)—puts forward the idea that global cities stand in as economic and political poles for the nations and that they constitute a network of interconnected interests.[4] Her idea, which had an immediate success, is that the future of the world is tied to the destiny and the growth of these global cities. Given her influence on the internal discussion of international organizations, urban globality became one of the indicators of the development of a country. If a country has at least one global city, a world city, it is destined to grow and provide prosperity. Even the European community, on a continent where the cities are contracting rather than expanding, has decided to finance only those projects that are in expanding metropolitan areas. The consequences are comical. In order to have financial backing, Caltanissetta, Enna, and Agrigento have pretended to be a unique metropolitan area.[5] Ten years later Sassen has corrected herself and admits that the devolution of the nations is still some way off and that perhaps a world made up of global cities is still to come. It doesn't matter. The supporters of bigness join in the chorus, among them the ever-present Rem Koolhaas, who sees in bigness the sense of an unstoppable development of capital for which he will be constrained—poor baby—to work. They say that the Chinese are realists because they understand that their unstoppable traction is hidden in the abnormal overdevelopment of their cities. Bigness envelops the world and turns it into something far less exciting but perhaps subtler. *Empire* by Negri and Hardt provides the opportunity for enthusiasts of radical politics to align themselves with the word of bigness.[6] What is greater than an empire, than a city that becomes a world capital and manifests itself as a unique organism?

Meanwhile, in California a strange drift of neo-Darwinism creates a thought that provides the background for some forward leaps of technology and the network. The internet, the web, becomes a real live organism in the minds of such people as Raymond Kurzweil, Stewart Brand, and Kevin Kelly,[7] and they quickly pass from a position of ecological militancy to a reformation of liberal thinking in a neo-Darwinistic key. The capitalist system, revised and fortified by computer technology, is an autopoietic organism, superseding individual reasons and any attempt at repression. It is really a true second nature. The distinction between *natura naturans* and *natura naturata* which Gregory Bateson took back from Bacon in *Mind and Nature* didn't make sense anymore.[8] (Bateson was part of the California world in the eighties.) The "Mind," be it the huge web, or the capitalistic system, or globalization and with it, global cities, becomes nature in the closest sense of the word. It is something that is *out of control*, as Kevin Kelly has said. We have to accept the times and the methods through which this nature is evolving and self-regulating. It is useless to oppose it. If we go along with it, we can encompass everything, a technology that can help humanity to free itself even from death. Kurzweil founded an institution which is working on immortality, achievable by overcoming deterioration and illness. It is biology applied to capital, giving life to a neoliberalism that is not that of the wicked Wall Street denizen wearing the characteristic black top hat, but that of the guru of Silicon Valley who rides a bicycle and sets up philanthropic foundations.

In this vein, the city no longer needs the country or nature, where the resources it depends on for its survival come from. The city is a self-regulating organism, however crude its movements and rejections may seem to be. Within its globality one can catch sight of slums and new poverty, wastelands, and even demonstrations in the streets. It has to do with becoming part of the healthy realism of those who look toward a prosperous future.

It has to be said that this new entity is in part pure ideology, self-fulfilling prophecy, publicity for a system that is by no means global, so it can convince itself that there is no way out. (This is nothing new, seeing that globalization is a phenomenon that continually appears throughout history.) In part it is a jump ahead of neoliberal thinking, its cohesion part of a universality which it borrows from the holism of eighties ecology.

Google, Facebook, Amazon, and Twitter are its Four Horsemen of the Apocalypse, ready to accompany us from here to eternity. Cities are the obvious corollary to their universality (otherwise why call them global?), cities promising to be the hub of ubiquity as well as entryways to a dematerialized geography.

Reality is quite a bit different. Instead of being the fruit of an inexorable logic of the global organism, what is happening to the city/country rapport comes from a very precise choice. The countrysides are removed from an organized use of feeding those who live there and in the surrounding area. The agriculturists will be thrown out by the politicians who favor the multinational seed and pesticide producers. Insert here the useless debates about genetically modified organisms (GMOs).

Even the World Bank is paying attention. You can read about it in the 2008 report of the International Assessment

of Agricultural Science and Technology for Development
(IAASTD), a project initiated by the World Bank, the first scientific evaluation of the global character of agriculture. Edited by
more than four hundred scientists from throughout the world,
the report maintains that GMOs do not play a useful role in
reaching the Millennium Development Goals or in eradicating
world hunger. Here are some of the reasons:

> The genetically modified herbicide-resistant soy cur-
> rently marketed produces a crop that is 10 percent lower
> than that from traditional varieties; extreme tempera-
> ture fluctuations have caused losses in cotton harvests
> in China; all the GMO products, even those developed
> by government research institutes, are controlled under
> the trademarks of a few multinationals. The trademarks
> add hugely to the cost of the seed. In the United States
> the price of genetically modified cotton has quadrupled
> during the past ten years.

The techniques of conventional reproduction, whether
traditional or modern, have a fundamental role in obtaining
long-term solutions for the food shortage crisis. They increase
the capability of plants to withstand unpredictable and various
changes in the weather due to climate changes.

Specific choices are at the base of the emptying of the
countryside, for example, the production of hydrocarbons
as a substitute for declining petroleum supplies. In 2007 the
United States shifted 54 million tons of corn to the production
of bioethanol, and the European Union used 2.85 million hectares to produce rapeseed and other grains for making biofuel.
If the same acreage had been allotted to the production of corn
and grain for alimentary purposes, an estimated harvest of 68
million tons of cereal would have been gathered, enough to
feed 373 million people for an entire year—the populations
of all of the 28 most underdeveloped countries of Africa put
together. The rush to hydrocarbons in international markets

has taken away agricultural land from the production of food, causing price jumps in basic foodstuffs, making grains much more expensive. Moreover, it is contributing to the destruction of rainforests, hastening climate change.

Speculation in raw materials is another factor related to the rise in food prices, because the speculators, who distanced themselves from other markets in decline, are constantly enriching themselves through futures pricing of raw materials. The growing demand for meat, as a result of the spread and assimilation of the western diet, is taking grains away from people in order to feed cattle. It has been estimated that if 50 percent of the populations of the EU countries and the United States substituted vegetables for half of their annual consumption of meat, the grain no longer destined to feed cattle would be enough to feed half of the undernourished peoples of the world.[9]

Climate change increasingly influences agriculture worldwide. Food security, especially in the poorest countries, is threatened by unpredictable changes in rainfall and by other frequent extreme weather events. As well, intensive agricultural practices contribute greatly to the emission of greenhouse gas, whether directly—for example by the use of fertilizers—or indirectly, as the result of the destruction of forests.

The most efficacious strategy for adapting to climate changes is through agriculture based on biodiversity. Data from different parts of the world demonstrate unequivocally that uniting different crops and varieties represents a reliable method for strengthening resistance to the unforeseen meteorological phenomena linked to climate change.[10]

The UN-Habitat report says little about all this. Urbanization is an unstoppable world trend. Which is opposed by antiurban reactionism. The myopia of the report is so marked that there is a gap between the relations of UN-Habitat and the most recent studies of the same international entities on the effect of urbanization on climate change.

The other shortsighted aspect is in the lack of significance given to the importance which the agriculture of subsistence farmers and small producers still has around the world. For the longest time agriculture has been the most practiced activity in the world. The global tendency toward urbanization has caused a decline in the percentage of small farmers with regard to the global population, nevertheless, their total number is increasing and is estimated to include approximately 2.6 billion people and that is 40 percent of the world population. It is the small farmers who produce a great part of the food consumed in the world. The great majority of them cultivate less than two hectares of land in rural areas but also in and around the cities themselves. Their number and their percentage with respect to the total population varies substantially from country to country and is very high in Asian and African regions afflicted by hunger. Small farmers occupy around 60 percent of the arable land area and they contribute in a manner consistent with the global production of food. In Africa 90 percent of agricultural production comes from small farms. If a high percentage of the rural population is bound up with agriculture and they draw their own sustenance from little plots of land, the entire sector is oriented toward subsistence, which makes the families implicated in it that much more susceptible to the various kinds of diseases, insect or rodent invasions, or climate changes, but also to indirect factors such as market fluctuations and the presence or absence of infrastructure.[11]

Small-scale agriculture and subsistence farming have traditionally been perceived as outdated and sloppy by the institutions and academies that decide agricultural policies. Investments to sustain this type of agriculture have progressively declined in the past decades to negligible amounts. With low accessibility and a minimum opportunity for acquiring help, small farmers and the community of small producers are not attractive partners for modern agribusiness, and they fall through the statistical cracks of government departments, rendering the general scenario of this report full of assumptions and false parameters.

Kuala Lumpur, Malaysia

Sweaty capitalism. Arriving here from much poorer Indonesia one understands the difference between some "parameters" still oriented toward a local vision of the problems and the opportunities and the parameters that are instead influenced by "elsewhere." Kuala Lumpur is struck with the rage that is called adjustment to world-class cities. As they put it in the little booklet produced at the expense of the municipality, in order for Kuala Lumpur to become a city adjusted to world standards, it needs to solve some problems: congestion, hygiene, and above all, to achieve great appeal as a brand name. To this end the city contracted a business trust to construct a financial district that would also become a symbol. In exchange for the opportunity to construct two towers, the highest in the city, the trust has offered to transform a part of the surrounding jungle into a park. The towers were assigned to the architect Cesar Pelli, who has made a kind of one-hundred-story Sagrada Família, with the two towers joined together by an unusable bridge—additionally supported for good measure by two crutches. But the city got its symbol. This is now the logo of Kuala Lumpur. A skyscraper in the midst of others in a city that has not solved but actually complicated the traffic problems is above all a typical "anti-tropical" solution in a magnificent tropical setting. Here becoming a world-class city means offering to strangers, investors, tourists, international personages, and local nouveaux riches merchandise that is not produced here but makes the shopping mall in the new towers look like the shopping malls all over the world, Marks & Spencer, Dolce & Gabbana, Prada, Kiehl's, Sony, Starbucks. Then, cover everything outside with concrete to sweep under the rug the fact that we are in a tropical city. Add a carpet of flyovers, ambitious monorails, and enormous new monuments to the Islamic nation, immense mosques, colored onion domes, soaring minarets. This abstract city has nothing to do with the rivers (which have been brutally channeled) that crisscross it and nothing to do with the jungle, which has been held off as far as possible and offered up as a "distraction." The result is a distancing from reality which projects the city among the requirements of the international jet-setters but pushes it away from the answer to local issues and opportunities. Here the tragic poverty of urban indigence and of the total anonymity of those who sleep on the sidewalks of the "popular" areas such as Chinatown and Indian Town, where the street life that is characteristic of tropical Asia is carved out. These little spaces become something new with respect to the past. In Asian cities life on the street and the organization of space means an informality, an atmosphere of trees, dust, a life between inside and outside of the houses, which sets a general tone for the whole city. There are cities whose construction has a temporariness that allows for climatic and functional adaptations. Here the cement spoils any possibility of adjusting to the logistics of present time and place. The people, who generally in Asian cities are protagonists, here become an anonymous crowd, crushed by the demand of international consumption and in competition with it, offering fake merchandise, prostitution, and "exotic" catering at knockdown prices. Even the cosmopolitan aspect of the city reveals itself to be somewhat abstract. In cities like Kuala Lumpur, the logic of separate contiguous spaces prevails: Indians in one place, Chinese in another, Malaysians in still another. A booklet published by the municipality refers to their great success in the relocation of a slum that was in the city center. Always using the logic of private enterprise, the city had entrusted the land to be urbanized to a business group if they also constructed housing into which the inhabitants of the slum could be relocated. With the same logic they entrusted an expert government agency with the task of issuing building permits to the company. Here, as in "world-class" cities, all the hopes of the public enterprises seemed to be lodged in the brick. Kuala is becoming an important financial center, and, above all, an important Islamic financial center. It attracts rich tourists from Arab countries who are looking to live there, at lower prices and in a much more humid climate, something that for many is nowadays unattainable in Dubai.

NOTES

1   Rem Koolhaas and Bruce Mau, "Bigness, or the Problem of Large," in *S, M, L, XL* (New York: The Monacelli Press, 1995), 494–516. Published in Italian in *Junkspace* (Rome: Quodlibet, 2006).

2   One can look at the reports of UN-Habitat, *State of the World's Cities 2012/2013, Prosperity of Cities,* available at http://mirror.unhabitat.org/pmss/listItemDetails.aspx?publicationID=3387; *State of African Cities 2014: Re-imagining Sustainable Urban Transition,* https://unhabitat.org/?mbt_book=state-of-african-cities-2014-re-imagining-sustainable-urban-transitions; *The State of Asian Cities 2010/11,* http://mirror.unhabitat.org/pmss/listItemDetails.aspx?publicationID=3078; *State of Latin American and Caribbean Cities 2012,* http://mirror.unhabitat.org/pmss/listItemDetails.aspx?publicationID=3386.

3   Roxana Waterson, *The Living House: An Anthropology of Vernacular Architecture in South East Asia, Singapore* (Oxford: Oxford University Press, 1990).

4   Saskia Sassen, *The Global City: New York, London, Tokyo* (Princeton, NJ: Princeton University Press, 2001); Sassen, *Cities in a World Economy*, 5th ed. (Los Angeles: SAGE, 2018).

5   The first intervention for the institution of a metropolitan city in Sicily is the regional law no. 9/86. The metropolitan area, however, is not a politically administered entity but rather a "method" of regarding the territory based on specific dynamics. The metropolitan area is an area surrounding an agglomeration or a conurbation, dependent on it for services, infrastructure, and economic dynamics such as commuting. In European politics the city is particularly present: one sees in that sense the documents for program projections 2014–2020 and the classifying criteria which inspired them (classifications which have defined the objectives "City" and "Internal Areas"). As far as literature on the specific theme of cities and European politics, see Fabrizio Barca, *Un'agenda per la riforma della politica di coesione,* https://www.scribd.com/document/38999657/Rapporto-Barca-traduzione-italiana-un-agenda-per-la-riforma-della-politica-di-coesione.

6   Michael Hardt and Antonio Negri, *Empire* (Cambridge, MA: Harvard University Press, 2001).

7   Kevin Kelly, *Out of Control: The New Biology of Machines, Social Systems, and the Economic World* (Cambridge, MA: Perseus Books, 1995); Raymond Kurzweil, *The Singularity Is Near* (New York: Viking, 2005); Stewart Brand, *The Clock of the Long Now: Time and Responsibility* (New York: Basic Books, 1999).

56   FRANCO LA CECLA

8   Gregory Bateson, *Mind and Nature: A Necessary Unity* (Cresskill, NJ: Hampton Press, 1979).

9   David Pimentel and Marcia Pimentel, "Sustainability of Meat-Based and Plant-Based Diets and the Environment," *American Journal of Clinical Nutrition* 78, no. 3 (2003): 6605–35; Vaclaw Smil, *Feeding the World: A Challenge for the Twenty-First Century* (Cambridge, MA: MIT Press, 2000).

10 Jessica Bellarby, Bente Foereid, Astley Hastings, and Pete Smith, *Cool Farming: Climate Impacts of Agriculture and Mitigation Potential* (Amsterdam: Greenpeace International, 2008).

11 Reyes Tirado, "Defining Ecological Farming," Greenpeace Research Laboratories Technical Note 04/2009, June 2009, http://www.greenpeace.org/international/Global/international/publications/agriculture/2011/Defining-Ecological-Farming-2009.pdf.

CHAPTER 6

Why Urban Planning Is in a Deadly Delay: The Environment

NOTHING DEMONSTRATES THE CATASTROPHIC SITUA-
tion in which cities find themselves as much as the environmental question. To such a point that looking at the scene in
its entirety really leads one to suspect a suicidal tendency in
mankind.[1] Why has the insane pattern of urban expansion,
energy consumption, and mobility developed in Europe and
the United States been adopted by the rest of the world whereas
in the places of its origin it is clearly destined to provoke only
negative effects and the destruction of both constructed and
natural habitats? Why has China followed the mistaken pattern
of urbanization and urban sprawl, of extended cities? Why has
automobile madness become the symbol of well-being when
all the evidence and good sense demonstrate that it is totally
counterproductive? Is it probable that humanity in its entirety
is about to be deluded for the nth time by the self-regulating
nature of neoliberalism, by consumer capitalism and real estate
investments? Who could believe anymore that cities are self-
regulating? Interviewing profound and intelligent historian
Gyan Prakash, author of *Mumbai Fables*,[2] a cultural history of
the megalopolis of Mumbai, I became aware that even he was
ensnared by the illusion of the city that in every case could overcome its "contradictions." I went to visit him at his home in
Andheri, a neighborhood of Mumbai facing the ocean. To my
question as to whether he thought that Mumbai was close to

collapse, he replied that for the last fifty years the prevailing note had been everyone announcing a catastrophe that then did not happen. Mumbai always manages to get out of it, to overcome its crises and rise again as a city with many problems to which it also has the solutions.

In truth, if Mumbai does not have a catastrophe of huge proportions happening to it, it does have a day-to-day catastrophe always present in the lives of its inhabitants, and it is the poor of the city who are the ones to feel its burden most. This characteristic is shared by many other megalopoli. Those who live on the air-conditioned twentieth floor and drive their own SUVs are no longer in touch with the physicality of life on the sidewalks and the streets, with those whose daily existence is suspended by personal tragedy and sickness, short life, infant mortality, violence, and desperation. The poor are paying the toll for the rich in the self-regulating capacities of the market.

We know that on the contrary the situation of the planet is at risk because of the weight of urbanization imposed on it. According to the Intergovernmental Panel on Climate Change (IPCC), urban areas contribute between 71 and 76 percent of the CO_2 emissions, due to energy usage and represent between 67 and 76 percent of the global energy used by the planet. And for those wishing to have data by geographical areas: "According to the International Energy Agency (IEA) the estimate of CO_2 emissions linked to cities talks of 69 percent for Europe, 80 percent for the United States and 89 percent for China."[3]

Today coping with the urban question means confronting climate change on the planet. Cities are often the first victims of climate change, but they are also the principle perpetrators, as the United States is finding out (finally motivating Obama and the Congress to become interested in it).

From the point of view of urban planning, it is outdated and too late. The urgency with which we should be moving is dampened by the slowness with which we are taking note of the abyss opening at our feet. We can no longer practice urban planning without taking into account the strongest measures to limit the catastrophic nature of cities.

As the IPCC report tells it:

> Urban density affects GHG [greenhouse gas] emissions in two primary ways. First, separated and low densities of employment, commerce, and housing increase the average travel distances for both work and shopping trips. These longer travel distances translate into higher VKT and emissions. Conversely, higher population densities, especially when co-located with high employment densities are strongly correlated with lower GHG emissions. In the United States, households located in relatively low density areas ($0-19$ households/km^2) produce twice as much GHG emissions as households located in relatively high density areas ($1,900-3,900$ households/km^2).[4]

Urban planning can turn out to be useful as a discipline that inspires new fundamental principles for the regulation of cities. Instead of cradling us in the promise of prosperity through urbanization, it can root out the dangerous blight. In that sense, cities as we know them now are no longer geared to what is happening. To stop or slow climate change, we have to rethink from the ground up a whole series of facts currently taken for granted. Interestingly, the IPCC report challenges the findings of the UN-Habitat report cited in the previous chapter, leaving serious doubts about the estimates for a successful urban future in those reports:

> While the UNDP (United Nations Development Program) has produced a global scenario on urbanization of the planet up to 2050, the studies suggest that the processes of urbanization vary according to the countries and the time periods taken into consideration. Moreover, the projections of the United Nations in

this field have contained gross errors of evaluation and have tended to overestimate urban growth, above all at the level of medium and small cities. . . . This implies that realistically by 2050 one could talk about the inferior levels of the increment of urbanization in India and China and the percentages are much more fluctuating and uncertain (between 38 percent and 60 percent for India and between 55 percent and 78 percent for China).

But setting up in opposition to urban triumphalism is not enough, we need to reform the way in which cities function today. First and foremost is the question of density. It is no longer possible to think that cities can exist where the distance traveled between home and work is two or three hours, whether by public transportation or private. When the inhabitants of San Francisco block the buses of the super-privileged from Silicon Valley who love to sleep in the city of hills but who work far from it, it signifies that a certain pattern is emerging even in the United States.

The Calthorpe Associates firm in Berkeley has put together an eight-point plan for China along these lines. But obviously it would also make a lot of sense to see them applied simultaneously in the United States.

Here are the eight principles of the plan:

1. Develop neighborhoods that promote walking
2. Prioritize bicycle networks
3. Create dense networks of streets and paths
4. Support high-quality transit
5. Zone for mixed-use neighborhoods
6. Match density to transit capacity
7. Create compact regions with short commutes
8. Increase mobility by regulating parking and road use

It is still a vision of the "garden city," and it is infuriating to think how Asian and Latin American cities had already been following the pattern, developing all-bike systems in Hanoi, Beijing, and Bombay, but then destruction arrived in the form of automobile traffic, in particular the individual car. Certain cities in Latin America have had collective systems of *camionetas*—minibus taxis—that provided inexpensive door-to-door transportation. (What is carsharing if not a return to this obvious solution?) It is as if the blight of the mistaken pattern were uncontrollable and had to be overcome by force. What *is* certain is that we can no longer turn away from density. Those in Italy who are preoccupied with "urban sprawl" have forgotten to condemn this insane pattern of land use. There should be strict judgments and more severe laws to avoid the devastation involved in the infinite spread of suburbs of Italian cities.

Renzo Piano, a sharp, on-the-ball person who was nominated a senator of the Italian Republic, has decided to donate his salary to the study of solutions for the suburbs. The problem is that the suburbs are an enormous mistake. It is rather like wanting to cope with the city of the future by saving the individual automobile.

The suburbs are the mistaken thinking of an urban plan that has mythologized the working condition while negating the city center instead. These strongholds of workers' sleeping quarters have quickly become the bugaboo of the "subordinate" classes and of immigrants today. Their mistaken character is not formal and has nothing to do with the design dimension or of the quality of the buildings. What is in question is the conceptual error of thinking that something such as the suburbs should ever be allowed to exist. Cities are not going to save themselves from catastrophe and climate change without extirpating the suburbs from existence. Suburbia contains a dangerous ideology, not very far removed from the myth that slums are a solution for cities. It creates false and dangerous identities, strips away citizenship from a majority of people, and presents them with the status of a population "in crisis." It is the kind

of thinking that slows down the necessity of taking action on
density and giving power back to a multifunctional city, and it
continues to perpetuate the idea that a residence can exist as a
separate function from living in the city.

There are cities that have understood this error and even as
they are providing "houses for everyone" they have made sure
that these are part of a richly functioning pluricentric tapestry.
For example, the story of planning in Singapore, all played out
on the gamble of occupying only 16 percent of the ground of
the tropical island on which five million inhabitants live. The
pattern could be criticized, but not the urgency with which it
was faced. It was understood that the stakes in play here were to
avoid pollution and the stupidity of individual vehicular traffic
and of long distances between different functional areas.

The other obvious thing cities will have to face up to is the
virtual disappearance of "anarchical" and "neoliberal" vehicular
traffic. Petroleum is rapidly becoming extinct, and its substi-
tutes can last only temporarily. In future scenarios the idea of
individual vehicular traffic is absurd, even for the automobile
industry. The pattern is already outdated today, and it is not by
chance that it is Google who wants to put their hands on the
innovations in this field. Within ten years cars will have to follow
standards of satellite control and of automatic driving. A good
part of the freeways that access the city resemble tracks into
which the traffic is channeled bestowing on the single driver the
power of the traffic jam. Google today is the largest producer
of geolocation systems used in vehicles. And they already have
prototypes on sale in three states in North America. The society
for French freeways is predicting a change of use of their own
property, from long-distance routes to service roads between
adjacent towns.

The lessening of the polluting power of buildings, through
the materials from which they are constructed, the lessening of
pollution due to heating and cooling systems, the use of renewable energy for 100 percent of urban needs—all this is not a

distant utopia but the goal already adopted by the municipalities most aware of the dangerous position in which they find themselves.[5] China is a country where the situation is so far beyond every supportable threshold that it has made its own the indications not from other governments but from a "militant" organization like Greenpeace, aligned forever against the use of coal as an energy source. China is a victim of coal, and anyone who lands in the milky smog of Beijing knows only too well that it is now an indelible and permanent fixture of the city. For the first time ever, China has this year reduced its carbon output by 2 percent and is attempting to move toward production that is less catastrophic for the environment.

Even in the case of the Calthorpe firm, the Chinese asked, as we have seen, for an advisory in the form of *Energy Foundation 2011 Annual Report*, for the cases of the urban areas of Kunming and Chongqing. The decisions made by the planning committee in China—to create new satellite cities, a new freeway, or an immense residential area—are much more far-reaching than those made in other countries of the world. Taken together, what appeared to be minor decisions in fact determine the lines of conduct for Chinese cities in the decades to come and probably even longer. More and more Chinese leaders are recognizing that, given the urgency, they can choose to do many things at one time: improve transportation, reduce carbon emissions, stimulate commercial activity, ameliorate the quality of the air, salvage arable land from building speculators, and sustain a more prosperous and integrated society. In Asia, Africa, and part of Latin America, it is also still possible to reverse tendencies.

Taxes on urbanization in developed regions are high, from 73 percent in Europe to 89 percent in North America, compared to 45 percent in Asia and 40 percent in Africa, and they correspond to the lower levels of economic development with respect to the urban transition achieved in Europe and North America. Even if the level of urbanization is still lower than that of Europe or North America, the urban population in Asia has increased by 2.3 billion from 1953 to 2010.

While the strongly urbanized areas in North America, Europe, Oceania, and Latin America continue to become more urbanized, the increase in population in these regions remains rather modest. On the other hand, urbanization in Asia and Africa, where the majority of the population is still rural, will be more significant. For these areas and for Latin America there is talk of a decrease in the rural population, which constituted 60 percent in 1950 but already only 30 percent in 2010, and it is projected that by 2050 it will decline by another 20 percent.

If, however, it becomes possible to intervene in these areas with policies of sustainable agriculture and small farmers, these tendencies can be circumvented and the disasters of the mythology of urban prosperity prevented.

Tashkent, Uzbekistan

It was to have been a purely instrumental stopover. I was told that I might meet Elizabeth, Bruce Chatwin's widow, in Tashkent and with her I would be able to reach Samarkand and the group of archeologists with whom we had appointments. The idea was to write a book about Chatwin in Afghanistan with Elizabeth and Maurizio Tosi, an archeologist who had been a friend of Bruce's. We were going there to explore the other stops along the Silk Road, and Samarkand was not to be missed. Elizabeth, however, was not going to arrive for twenty-four hours. I had also been told that Tashkent was a dangerous city, scarcely out from under Soviet domination and in the midst of the torments of the new republic after the fall of the wall. I dropped off my luggage in a low-class hotel near the airport and started on my rounds. I knew absolutely nothing about the city and I spoke neither Russian nor Turkmeno. But this city of wide streets bordered by terrace housing with an air of the thirties had a fascination that beckoned me onward. On foot I arrived at the part constructed directly from Soviet planning, which sought to invent an "Asian" style for the cities it had conquered with the shedding of a quantity of local blood. The USSR had had to subjugate courageous leaders and their subjects, and it had not been an easy task. The tree-lined boulevards, the cleanliness of the sidewalks and the parks, the general air of care offered by the city gave the image of a gallant attempt to impose upon a city of nomads the mark of a centralist and powerful state. However, the effect was not unpleasing. Tashkent had effectively the air of a capital city and a refinement that did not inharmonious with its oriental attributes. A few signs emerged as evidence of a local substrate: a bear was tied up right outside one of the stations on the metro. This station, completed midway through the seventies, had a paradoxical look. Huge mosaics illustrated the feats of Yuri Gagarin, the first man in space, dressed as if he were a potentate from Central Asia, a Tamerlane, or a Genghis Khan. All of it lit with luxurious chandeliers, like a direct descendant of its Moscow counterpart.

If you press on through the city, you come across open-air markets with everything under the sun, the same watermelons that Bruce had photographed and that originate right here in this land of steppes and plains, cotton and fruit, peaches, melons, pears, and every kind of honey. Continuing to amble around the quarter, I ended up in the area that was truly Uzbek, that constituted the mahalle, with lots separated by mud walls. A very diverting sight, and a color so different from the asphalt of the Soviet city. Seeking to spy into the quadrangles of mud through the wooden doors, I discovered that there were marble pavements and that frequently there was a high-powered car parked in the courtyard. The luxury was reserved for intimates and outside there was a sense of a nomad identity. Now a new nomenklatura in Uzbekistan wants a return to the traditions that were violently opposed by the Soviets: language, mode of dress, customs, songs, wedding rituals, and rites of passage.

The connection of the two souls, the Uzbek one and the Russian one in devolution were in some public places that I discovered much later at the end of the day, when I had already wandered around for hours, fascinated by the variety and complexity of Tashkent. There were the discotheques filled with boys and girls a few steps away *from where camels were being given water and kiosks where they were selling pins, caps, and uniforms with the hammer and sickle on them and the CCCP symbol.*

When, famished, I reached an area with small houses not far from the airport, I found another component: Koreans and their restaurants. Asking around on the street for information on where to eat, I was directed there, bearing in mind that if I wanted to, I could eat dog, which they prepare very well. I preferred the little Armenian places, where the food arrives as a series of little plates to pick on, preparing the stomach for the more substantial mutton.

NOTES

1   It is what one reads between the lines in the *Synthesis Report (Summary for Policymakers)* from IPCC on climate change. Intergovernmental Panel on Climate Change, November 2014, http://www.ipcc.ch/report/ar5/syr/.

2   Gyan Prakash, *Mumbai Fables* (Princeton, NJ: Princeton University Press, 2010).

3   IPCC, Working Group III; material available at http://www.ipcc-wg3.ac.uk/; in particular see *Climate Change 2014: Mitigation of Climate Change*, available at https://www.ipcc.ch/report/ar5/wg3/, especially chap. 8, *Transport*; chap. 9, *Buildings*; and chap. 12, *Human Settlements, Infrastructure, and Spatial Planning.*

4   IPCC, *Mitigation of Climate Change*, 952.

5   Today it is calculated that the transformation of a city's building property, with lower energy consumption and with heating and cooling systems linked to renewable energy, cuts down 70 percent of the emissions of CO_2 and its contribution to global warming by cities.

CHAPTER 7

Lies and Lost Opportunities for Involvement

I ALREADY HEAR THE OBJECTIONS: "WE MIGHT AGREE with your criticisms of urban planning, but you are forgetting the participatory processes" and "Your view of the discipline is out of date: nowadays there is no regulatory plan that does not allow for means of interaction with the citizens, and there are studies and agencies to take care of that very thing."

I know: involvement was a rising star of great brilliance during the years of Jane Jacobs and advocacy planning. She saw moments of glory even when the archistars stood pat on the process of design, from Christopher Alexander to Herman Hertzberger to Aldo Van Eyck to Giancarlo De Carlo himself.[1] In England and the United States involvement gave rise to practices and specific methods that Marianella Sclavi has described in her books and that were then imported to Italy.[2] Avventura Urbana was and is an agency in Italy that concerns itself professionally with organizing participatory actions. This is all well and good, but my impression is that they have as yet barely scratched the surface of urban planning as such. This should soon become a separate undertaking Just as there exist specialists in floor tiling, so there exist participators. They are being used by administrations and local authorities, as well as by big design firms, to mediate the relationship between the project and the consumers. They become facilitators of consensus, or at any rate negotiators between the demands of the population and the decisions of the planners. It is the great field of public advocacy, where trained professionals come to take care of the interests of the populations impacted by a project and become their spokespeople. It is the very vast field of social filtering between users ever less accustomed to asserting their rights directly and planners who do not want to be directly implicated. Certainly it serves to muffle the conflicts, a species of professional cushioning between divergent interests. The problem is that in this specialized filtering function everything pieces itself back together again in such a way that nothing changes very much in the passiveness of the residents and in the traditional methods of the planners.

The effective result is that urban planning continues with its methods and representations and the residents continue to think that they do not have any true access to the "language" of planning and projects, unless some social operator appears to explain it to them. It is a bit of a consensus trap and the operators involved know from experience how it feels to be suspended between a true communicative function and one that is often purely advertising, especially if they are being paid by public or private businesses.

We've been talking about it and doing it for at least sixty years, and meanwhile powerful resources which would have really been able to reform the method of doing urban planning have been pushed off into a corner. I am referring to the example of social impact assessment, which even though approved by the European Community as a parallel practice to that of environmental impact assessment has not had the same application and the same contractual force.

In 1983 the sociologist Roy T. Bowles defined social impact assessment as an attempt to restore a scientific aspect to public policies, furnishing information about the predictable results of a project, establishing trajectories for a possible beneficial social change, and indicating how the success or failure of the project or of planning policy could be monitored through the application of the scientific methodology used in the social sciences.[3]

In general, the impact assessment is the process that identifies the future consequences of an action during its development or in the amplification phase of the proposal. In the case of social impact assessment, what is defined by international legislation and by the researchers of the discipline as one of the principal subsectors in the evaluation of the impact, is the process of identification and of analyses of future consequences of an action, up and running or simply in proposal, linked to the individuals, to the communities and the macrosocial systems.[4]

The definition of the term "social impact" given by Thomas Dietz is significant, as it underlines that social impact is what indicates an amelioration or a deterioration of the well-being of people or that significant positive change in an aspect concerning the community.[5]

The interesting aspect of social impact assessment is that it digs into the decision-making processes and not just into participation. It casts doubt on the comprehensiveness of the urban planning structure and forecasts that it may be offset by the methodology of social analyses. In short, it implies not a "professionalism of the report," but a professionalism in the reading of the report. The former is always exposed to the risk of manipulation of the consensus and negotiations, the latter claims that the decision-making processes are subject to social control. The difference is noteworthy for those who believe, as I do, that some professional practices have to change but still have to stay within a certain competence. I am still very uncomfortable with the practices of negotiation—at least in those cases where it is not clear who is paying the negotiators. Moreover, the social impact assessment is an attempt to reinterpret a good part of the settlement processes as opposing forces and of favoring an idea of improving the quality of housing ahead of other parameters.

In this direction the most recent researches conducted as part of the of social impact assessment carried out in Australia, the United Kingdom, and the United States have created an autonomous scientific methodology, gaining a relevant independence with regard to other impact assessments, sharply outlining limits and contributing to an important theoretical development of the discipline. In light of these more recent analyses we can define social impact assessment as the process which analyzes (predicts, evaluates, and reflects) and *manages* the intentional and unintentional consequences of interventions (policies, plans, projects, and other social activities) and processes of social changes, on the human environment, with the objective of provoking or inducing the creation of a more sustainable biophysical and human environment.[6] The important implications of this definition are that:

- the social impact assessment provides for adaptive management of the impacts of projects and policies (as if providing for prediction, mitigation and monitoring) and therefore demands to be included or at least considered from the inception of an eventual planning of a policy or a project;
- it is a process which can be applied to a vast scale of interventions and be assumed by a vast range of social players, not just within the development of the normative "framework";
- the interconnection between the biophysical and social impacts is considered implicit;
- the general objective of the advice furnished is to lead to the construction of a sustainable world and social and ecological sustainability concepts must be considered to be related to one another.[7]

In short, with respect to participation, the social impact assessment implies involving private or public planning entities in a different manner of interpreting an intervention and, above all, of a different timing. In fact, if that is the case, it is a kind of both proactive and successive monitoring of a completed project. What is the impact of something such as Expo 2015? What is the impact on historic Harlem in Manhattan of the redoubling of the size of the Columbia campus? What is the impact of the erection of a high-speed train station in the outskirts of Barcelona in a high-density, socially compact neighborhood?[8]

Social impact assessment provides a reading of the inhabited territory that does it justice, treating social issues not as a tabula rasa but as something to be reckoned with on a par with architectural and urban preexistence. Social impact assessment "materializes" the body of the citizens and their connections with the place and among themselves and makes visible that reciprocity that constitutes housing and its culture. Inside social impact assessment a specific interpretation is attributed precisely to the added value of the home, that being in one particular place makes it more precious and the invitation to others to join in becomes more tempting. And then there is the problem of gentrification, which cannot be addressed in a banal and mechanical manner.

Housing itself creates a form of gentrification, because it makes a part of the city safer, more social, more filled with offers of networks in the neighborhood, petty trade and the general management of daily life. Perhaps slums that have been degraded with time become transformed by those who live there into places that well-to-do classes and castes can think of moving into. What is banally forgotten is that the inhabitants themselves are provoking the gentrification, because exactly like everyone else they aspire to improve the everyday conditions of their own existence. Often, as happens in the slums, this improvement is coupled with the entry of an impoverished middle class, who in relocating see an opportunity for saving and integrating into a less competitive network. But the same story also goes for marginal neighborhoods, deteriorated suburbs, and abandoned historic centers.

Social impact assessment can make interpreting these processes an interesting key to urban dynamics and something more than pure anti-gentrification recriminations. It is clear that what interests me here is the cognitive character of social impact assessment and its fallout on the play of opposing forces in a city. But I would like to subject this game to the purely syndical and demanding logic of the interests in the conflict. Often this reasoning contributes only to a city effect characterized by fragmented interests, to an idea of urban cohabitation as pure combat managed by representatives of differing and opposing minorities and communities (although not by them directly, but by professional combatants). This vision has nothing to do with the possibility of creating cities that offer to those who live there a sense of togetherness and of shared interests. The syndical logic of the fragmentation of interests is a logic often far removed from the interpretation of real processes and their possible production of an impact on a city.

However, we are only at the inception of a disciplinary story in which social impact assessment integrates itself in a decisive manner into urban processes. In 2008 the European Commission authorized The Evaluation Partnership (TEP) of London to delve into the nature and practices of social impact assessment. The study, produced by TEP with the collaboration of the Center for European Policy Studies and issued in June 2013, offers an account of how this particular kind of evaluation is accomplished and from which member states of the European Union it emanates. The objective is to "describe, compare and analyse the different ways in which social impact assessment is currently carried out in the EU Member States, and to identify recommendations for the implementation of effective social impact assessment systems and for effective social impact analysis."[9]

The study analyzed ten member states where social impact assessment is well developed or had particularly interesting results. It then compared the methods used by different states, studying thirty concrete examples of its application. The most obvious thing demonstrated by the report is that social impact assessment is still in its infancy. Where it is carried out, it is often less well developed than environmental or financial impact assessments. The examples of assessment which present an in-depth analysis of social impacts are few and far between; where they do exist they are often conducted on policies and plans with specific predetermined social objectives.

In spite of the European system of impact assessment requiring that every national government include the social impact assessment, in Italy not only has it never been included in any analysis of impact assessment up until now but, unlike in other member states, no national guidelines exist that define the nature and the objectives of social impact assessment. The lack in Italy of a deep and coherent theoretical amplification, as well as the nonexistence of national guidelines of a struc-tured framework, is such that it even drew the attention of the analysts, who in the official report delivered to the European Commission underlined: "In Italy, where there is no strong culture of planning, evaluating and monitoring, IA [impact assessment] has not yet been mainstreamed into policy making, and is reportedly still perceived by most officials as just another layer of bureaucracy. The fact that in Italy IA reports are not made public removes another potential incentive for producing high quality IAs."[10]

As a whole, social impact assessment, if applied, could serve to redevelop part of the urban planners' work, even though the danger is strong that it represents further bureaucratization. Because if there is an aspect of urban planning which is even stronger, it is that of surrounding itself with all the obstacles and bottlenecks of bureaucracy, making room for the regula-tions and codicils and totally forgetting that the society with which it is concerned is a dynamic and living organism. One often forgets about the bureaucracy of urban planning, yet its language, the mass of maps and statistics, of graduated scales and legends, corresponds to a language for initiates very dear to all disabling professions,[11] which separates inhabitants and regulators with an ever-growing gap.

Shanghai, China

We are facing each other on the parapet of the Bund, the colonial style riverfront of Shanghai, on the great Blue River, which takes its name from Huangpu. Barges, huge ships carrying containers, multi-tiered motorboats for tourists are passing by. On the turbulent waters of the river, which until fifty years ago was host to junks and sailboats, the skyscrapers of Pudong are reflected, chaotic, flashy as a collection of overgrown cigarette lighters. The young Chinese urban planner who is accompanying me, Ren Yeaung, is part of a group, Urban China, who are observing the rapid expansion of Chinese cities with a very critical eye. But when I ask him if he doesn't think that what we are seeing is at the end of the day the pursuit of the skyscrapers of America, he replied, "No, it is Hong Kong." And he is right, here the symbol of growth is no longer America, but the golden goose of Chinese capitalism, the autonomous Hong Kong, loved and held dear by the current regime and loved to death by all the Chinese who want to be part of the vertiginous growth of the country.

Ren showed me with pride a photo of Pudong twenty years ago, a peninsula of earth on the river, made up of fields, fishing rods, and marshy gorges. Pudong is the symbol of change for Shanghai, of what this city has conquered in order to become one of the most important cities in the country. When it was founded by the English used it to import the laws of Albion to the declining Celestial Kingdom. Here the English imposed the opium trade at gunpoint, so that the city became the center for its consumption and distribution. Along the same river that we are looking at thousands of sampans and junks traveled, hosting onboard opium dens and brothels. Then there was the revolution that exploded right here in resistance to the Japanese occupation and then for the elimination of the Imperial Dynasty and the proclamation of the Republic. And here the Communist Party held its most important conferences, bringing Mao and Maoism to power. Yet after the Revolution the city failed to renew itself and had to wait for the changes imposed by Deng Xiaoping, the attitude that said, "Get rich; it doesn't matter what the color of the cat is, black or white, the important thing is that it catches rats," that gave a role of primary importance back to Shanghai.

Today Shanghai has twenty-three million inhabitants, and every night thousands of immigrants arrive from the country. Shanghai is the symbol of socialist capitalism and the countryside is nowadays the symbol of backwardness, and that is why today there are three hundred million peasants in China who have become urbanized. Ren told me about the provisional settlements and barracks, on the borders of the city, about country people who are constrained to recycle anything they can find in the waste facilities in the outskirts and who are constantly being chased away again. But the influx appears to be unstoppable.

If I turn toward the Bund I see a really elegant croisette, the grand palaces of the one-time opium magnates, like Sassoon and Jardine, nowadays converted into luxury hotels and boutiques of international fashion houses. One comes here to be photographed with family because this is the symbol of what China has made of itself. If at one time under Mao the emphasis was on the suzhi, the authenticity of the peasant class, bearer of the revolutionary quality consisting of jianku puso, "bitter eating and simple living," today that same authenticity has become the patrimony of the urban class capable of nengzhen huihua, producing, and above all, consuming "authentically." The same expression, suzhi, "authenticity," is attributed to noncounterfeit merchandise, to real Guccis, Pradas, and Nikes. The urban classes and the party look with suspicion on the peasant world, accused of being outdated, subjected to the corruption of local bureaucrats, and above all thrown into turmoil because today the peasants are very discontented with the direction the country has taken. For them there is only the possibility of having to decide between the countryside where one is unable to live anymore and the city that doesn't want them there.

Shanghai is a monster made up of apartment buildings that are all exactly alike. You scarcely leave the center and you are in the suburbs. It is the Soviet model for living, squalid, identical, leveling. Anna Laura Govoni, an Italian architect who is here studying the mechanisms of socialization, shows me however that there still persists in the center the pattern of courtyards and low houses, those shikumen that are just now becoming fashionable but that in many parts of the city, especially in the elegant and tree-lined French concession, maintain a characteristic popularity. The clue, she shows me, is the inveterate habit of hanging out the laundry, a habit totally detested by the government, that the people of Shanghai bring with them even when they are relocated by force into sixty-story buildings. Looking out of the windows, one sees enormous networks of metal and bamboo that allow them to hang their clothes out to dry even on the forty-fifth floor. I walk back from the Bund toward the old city. And a few blocks from the chic riverbank boulevard appears the poor and the poverty-stricken city, filled with street markets, people eating ravioli and lacquered duck, fish heads, and fermented tofu. It is a feast of colors for the eye, but the density of living here, the overcrowding in the houses and the courtyards, speaks of an extreme poverty where one fends for oneself until being evicted on twenty-four hours' notice because of demolition and as one crosses the markets they look like patches of rubbish and ruin.

This is a country assaulted by spasms and horrifying waves, a place where globalization and modernization have radicalized the differences of opportunity, but also made individualists emerge, as is recounted in a beautiful book, Factory Girls, by a Chinese-American anthropologist, Leslie T. Chang.[12] Mobility throughout the country has given more autonomy to women than to men, because here it is the women who have always taken care of everything, and they are also able to change the situation if necessary. They have the courage to move, to risk their own lives in Shenzhen and, for those who make it, in Hong Kong—Fruit Chan portrays it in a beautiful film, Durian Durian, the story of a country girl who goes to become a prostitute in Shenzhen and who then returns to the province from whence she came. Nobody there knows what she went to do in Shenzhen, but she is torn between two incompatible identities. Or else, as Leslie T. Chang recounts, they are simply jumping from one factory to another where the conditions are better. It is a complicated country, immense, *like this city, but full of personal stories and new collective histories for us to lend heart and ear to.*

NOTES

1   Christopher Alexander et al., *A Pattern Language* (Oxford: Oxford University Press, 1977); Alexander, *The Oregon Experiment* (Oxford: Oxford University Press, 1975); Herman Hertzberger, *Space and the Architect: Lessons for Students in Architecture* (Rotterdam: 010 Publishers, 1991); Aldo Van Eyck, *The Playgrounds and the City* (Amsterdam: NAi Publishers, 2008); Franco Boncuga, *Conversazioni con Giancarlo De Carlo su Architettura e Libertà* (Milan: Eleuthera, 2013).

2   Marianella Sclavi, ed., *Avventure Urbane. Progettare la città con gli abitanti* (Milan: Eleuthera, 2002).

3   Roy T. Bowles, "Social Impact Assessment in Small Communities: An Integrative Review of Selected Literature," *Canadian Journal of Sociology/ Cahiers canadiens de sociologie* 8, no. 3 (1983): 349–51.

4   Henk A. Becker, "Social Impact Assessment," *European Journal of Operational Research* 128, no. 2 (2001): 311–21.

5   Thomas Dietz, "Theory and Method in Social Impact Assessment," *Sociological Inquiry* 57, no. 1 (1987): 54–69.

6   Frank Vanclay, *Social Impact Assessment: Contributing Paper for the World Commission on Dams* (Cape Town: World Commission on Dams, 2010).

7   Angelo Imperiale, *Epistemology of Complexity and Social Impact Analysis for Healthy Community Informatics Project*, CIRN Prato Community Informatics Conference, November 9–11, 2011.

8   Franco La Cecla, *Against Architecture* (Oakland: PM Press/The Green Arcade, 2012).

9   TEP-CEPS (The Evaluation Partnership and Center for European Policy Studies), *Study on Social Impact Assessment as a Tool for Mainstreaming Social Inclusion and Social Protection Concerns in Public Policy in EU Member States*, prepared for DG Employment, Social Affairs and Equal Opportunities of the European Commission, June 2010, page 3, available at https://ec.europa. eu/social/main.jsp?catId=89&langId=en&newsId=935.

10 TEP-CEPS, *Study on Social Impact Assessment*, 44.

11 Ivan Illich, *Disabling Professions* (London: Marion Boyars, 1977); Franco La Cecla, *L'eredità di Ivan Illich* (Milan: Medusa Editions, 2012).

12 Leslie T. Chang, *Factory Girls: From Village to City in a Changing China* (New York: Spiegel and Grau, 2008).

CHAPTER 8

Against the Slogans of Urban Planning Glamour

IN THE PAST THIRTY YEARS EPISTEMOLOGICAL POVERTY and the inefficacy of urban planning in confronting the actions of the real estate sector have been compensated by the plentiful invention of slogans: *creative cities, creative factories, smart cities, resilient cities, nature cities*, and ultimately *open-source cities*. At the end of the day this habit of "sloganizing" urban planning is even more outdated if the departments of sustainable cities are wasting themselves in the faculty of architecture and planning. We have already seen how the idea of sustainability has become a key word, a magic word so hackneyed as to be completely devoid of content. It's a little like the gross national product sung in the "ecological" key. But even ecology has different approaches. A product from a multinational company that exploits its workers or from a monoculture that starves the peasants can still be sustainable. In the concept of *sustainability* there is the usual crasis due to the fact that its Anglo-American nature is all too explicit and however it is translated it is a ridiculous neologism that comes across as self-justifying. In the Italian language, in order to "sustain something," one needs to have a point of view, and sustainability is not an objective value.

Unfortunately, this tradition of making slogans expands and impoverishes itself conceptually with the "launch" of creative cities. Richard Florida has built a fortune on it, suggesting right and left (when he was consulted by municipalities who wanted "placement" in the World Cities of the world) that all that was needed was the right mix of creative classes and the game was won.[1] Creative cities are the setting for a new middle class linked to the information revolution combined with creative expertise, from artists to stylists, from video makers to curators. This mixture needed a few dot-commers, a few gays, a few taggers, a few designers, a few hipsters, a few geeks, and a few gurus. New cities would be born on a new vanguard capable of giving life to a third sector, transforming entire cities into "creative" laboratories. Too bad that the crisis arrived and places like Barcelona, San Francisco, Reykjavik, Bangalore, and Ouagadougou have demonstrated that perhaps the creative class is nothing more than a part of the middle class and even of the lower middle class, the petty bourgeoisie, and if the middle class is driven out, the reasons for creativity will disappear. The idea of an informal economy tied to a world of art and design is so little aligned with the way the economy progresses in Silicon Valley, it ends up killing its own creative neighborhoods, in San Francisco just as in Milan or in Bangalore. The problem with creative cities is that they are linked at a precise historic moment that is fortuitous for yuppies and hipsters, but the same people who have created enormous fortunes, like Zuckerberg and the founders of Google, have moved on to something else, to become corporations and not a "creative tapestry." One has only to read *The Circle* by Dave Eggers or leaf through a few years of *Wired* to be aware of this.[2] What should be a melting pot of productive fantasy has finished up becoming a monopoly that has destroyed the precarious world of creative people. It has destroyed the music world, it is destroying publishing, and is poised to destroy other sectors, such as research, with the monopoly of washed-up popularization for TED-style scientific innovations. It is enough to follow what is happening in San Francisco, where the arrival of the techie population of Silicon Valley has tripled prices in the city, driven out artists, writers, and families, diminished the multi-ethnicity of neighborhoods like the Mission, and caused real and true revolts. People in San Francisco block the buses of the privileged that carry the rich commuters from the city to their "creative" places in Mountain View or Redwood City. All of it is tied in with the presumed idea of the democracy of the information revolution. Amazon defends itself from its attackers by claiming that they supply cheap books for everyone, obviously hiding the fact that they are destroying publishing and the possibility of living by writing. And the same thing is true of music-streaming platforms, which have devastated the world of the CD and have literally put musicians out on the street. The effect is contrary to the promise: instead of having a creative class, only the best-sellers and the superstars are surviving. For everyone else it is starvation. TED has become the place for a performance that favors science and research and the low level of its democratic nature has been denounced by several of its ex-protagonists who have witnessed the censoring of their videos.[3]

Lees, Slater, and Wyly reflect on the phenomenon of the seductive power of Richard Florida's "creative cities" and on his theses of "civic leaders scattered throughout the world" and maintain that from Singapore to London, from Dublin to Auckland, from Memphis to Amsterdam even to Providence and to Green Bay, cities have paid with cold, hard cash to hear the new creativity creed, to learn how to attract and nurture operators of creativity and how to evaluate the latest hipsterization strategies. Peck maintains that Florida's theses "launch" urban competitiveness as economic and cultural creativity, constituting a seductive narrative for policy makers, administrators, and politicians in an ever-more-crowded market of fast policy, characterized by "traveling truths" and "portable technocratic routines."[4] Learning how to make "creative cities" depends on the exposure of a number of actors and spaces in a series of conferences, websites, and blueprint posters announcing political projects. For Peck the success of Florida's traveling strategies lies partly in its promotional capacity and in the ability of the presenter, but it should all be seen in the context of a more comprehensive agenda identified by David Harvey as urban entrepreneurialism that is reflected in a growing number of consultants,[5] who are offering themselves to city mayors and political leaders in the form of public-private coalitions, to promote an urban environment for creative young people, tourism and an area of gentrification for new investors.[6]

It is the same problem that today faces the supporters of open-source architecture, convinced that the net is a democratic organism and that one does not play monopoly or oligopoly on it. The verb Google is so strong it has convinced everyone that they are dealing not with a vertical top-down management but a truly open and democratic meeting. And certainly Facebook or Twitter could have helped some popular processes, but it would be a grave error to exchange the means for the substance. Democracy is playing out in the streets as never before, and the network is an increasingly simplistic simulation of the streets. Ratti, who today supports crowd sourcing and open-source architecture, seems to be unaware that the debate on the democratic nature of the web is ever stronger.[7] And it is not by chance that only the TED award-winning part of Cameron Sinclair's work is known. But the enormous body of work "in the field" that is not on the website of Architecture for Humanity is not known.[8]

Perhaps the most intuition-rich and content-poor concept is that of *smart cities*,[9] computerized and technological cities where all the problems are resolved by intelligent machines. It is an old nineteenth-century dream of which Jules Verne was one of the founding fathers. The future is in the hands of the robots and whatever concerns the city there is no problem that cannot be addressed by the application of an appropriate technology. Smart cities rely on a bunch of experts for traffic, crime, the environment, and civic participation. Everyone can come in, the important thing is to be convinced that cities are *machines à habiter.* Behind smart cities in the long run is a professional category that wants to make a clean sweep of the old urban planners and set themselves up as a new science for the management of urban functioning. The cases cited of smart cities frequently resemble one another closely: one starts with Curitiba in Brazil and ends up with the new model neighborhoods in Stockholm. Very little emerges about the true body of the inhabitants, the lives they lead, of "urgency and necessity," as Unni Wikan would say, quoting Pierre Bourdieu. Cities should be little boxes easy to make function with the appropriate cocktail of experts and algorithms. In a recent collection *Gli algoritmi del capitale* edited by Matteo Pasquinelli,[10] one can read the substance behind this discourse, the Keynesian idea of control, or rather self-control, of capital, and of the big market. Today algorithms promise us the appropriate and neutral solution for each and every one of our problems.

Smart assumes the aspect of yet another badly translated Anglo-American expression. More than "intelligent cities," it would be better to translate it as "cunning cities."

You might think that Florida has ultimately replaced Rem Koolhaas and his "portable kit for every city." But there is also evidence that today urban planning has been reduced to "revitalization projects": how to turn cities into Expo settings, European cultural capitals, and centers for the World Cup or the Olympics, as if it were not possible to have a normal administration of a city, based on its energies, to furnish to its inhabitants a "normal," fitting quality of life. Perhaps it was actually Barcelona which opened the floodgates of this run-up to cities that had to "place themselves" in the international rankings.

All these slogans and these efforts ignore or obscure the real issue of the life of a city, that interplay between public and private which today is more and more flawed. The proposed Lupi/Realacci law,[11] which is about to be passed in Italy, with almost no opposition from professionals such as architects, engineers, and urban planners,[12] provides for the creation of a decision-making capacity in which private people—meaning real-estate and financial entrepreneurs—can decide the destiny of a city with equal weight as institutions. The Lupi/Realacci law (not by chance proposed by an ex-environmentalist) sells off Italian land to a construction group for "renewal of urban heritage" which allows private people to pay taxes for the damage done to the environment and to the historical centers and expropriate a large part of the control from the public bodies.[13] The new law even has provisions for the expulsion of inhabitants who smack of good regime policies. "Landlords or tenants of properties subject to urban renewal (up to and including demolition and reconstruction) shall be housed in newly constructed buildings 'as needed on a temporary or permanent basis.'" (Art. 17, c. 10).

Add to this the fact that the whole landscape can be declined in the form of an exchange between private and state-owned areas offered as collateral for the same. "The contribution may be substituted, subject to agreement with the community, for a compensatory transfer of public use areas, for the construction of new permanent natural systems whose hedgerows, fields, woods, wetlands are made available for ecological and environmental use, such as footpaths and bicycle lanes." (Art. 2, c. 3). This gives no indication of whether the title of the areas goes to the community or remains with the construction company or of who pays for the construction work.[14] As the icing on the cake, the law declares: "Whoever illegally occupies any building without title may not ask for the residence to be connected with public services in relation to the said building and the issued acts in violation of such ban are null and void to the extent of the law."

All this in a country where tens of thousands of vacant or abandoned apartments are occupied in the absence of a policy that would offer low-cost housing, and in the total absence of a plan for making use of abandoned properties. It is a war declared by the property moguls on the newly impoverished, and brilliantly maintained by the ex-environmentalists.

It is the Milan-ization of Italy. Milan has never had a zoning plan or a public plan for its own future. Each of its new quarters

and developments has been determined by the huge property
speculators and by their dreams of "satellite cities" for the rich.
The ultimate wave for the Expo is nothing less. How do you sell
the public on something like City Life or the "vertical forest,"
represented by two skyscrapers with trees on the balconies?
On something that goes against every public interest? It is the
failure of urban planning which for years has fought for a role in
planning and land protection but has never understood the way
things are changing. In the absence of the devolution of a strong
state and institutions equipped with resources and powers, the
only true power of decision-making is that of rich private individuals. Indeed, in the meantime no other instrument has been
created that is not purely partisan or consensual to empower the
citizens. Entrusting the future of Italian cities to the (few and
reactionary) ideas of property developers or, worse, to financiers, comes disguised as economic realism but instead provokes
only disasters even within the brick-and-mortar economy. The
wholly Italian problem is the clash between institutions and the
economy (of speculation) and the absolute lack of any stagecraft
in the dependent citizens (who put their trust in their elected
representatives and are promptly betrayed by them).

Today the sprinkling of "environmentalism" is back, and
even in Milan, one hears the ultimate slogan: *resilient cities*.
What I want to say is very vague. One goes from the idea that
the environment can be saved by trees planted on balconies by
Stefano Boeri in his private vertical forest to an idea of "resistance," of continuity, of directions taken on loan from slow food
and slowness as corollary passwords. Even here the translation
is ridiculous: "resiliente" in Italian doesn't mean anything and
in the translation it is supposed to mean flexible and resistant at
the same time. What could it imply? The capacity for adaption?
Long-term plans? Or simply the inhabitants' patience in putting
up with everything being done to their heads?

And what if instead we were to wrench back the super-
outdated concept of urban propriety?

Maybe it is the only way to defend ourselves from the screeching of the sloganeers. Valerio Paolo Mosco says:

> A completely obsolete expression in urban planning and architecture is propriety. Not only obsolete but so irritating to the reigning culture that it has become taboo. But still, without propriety the purpose for collective planning vanishes completely. The concept of propriety implies, as do all fundamental expressions, a philosophical reflection rather than a sociological one. Propriety is what upholds Kant's morality and the sense of limit that each one of us gives himself when relating to others and in self-reflection.
>
> To cite Max Weber, it is the moment of synthesis between the ethic of ideas and that of responsibility; its product is a collective accord that pertains more to behavior than to laws, more to morals than ethics. A culture ever more obsessed with consensus, with the myth of pop accessibility and at base contrary to the sense of limit, has delegitimized propriety. The fact is, as Roger Scruton rightly affirms, beauty bases itself on the concept of propriety, especially in urban planning and architecture. The pursuit of propriety is tiring and frustrating: propriety does not guarantee success in the media, doesn't attack and seduce the middle-class aesthetic. It finds space only in daily life and not in the representation of itself. Propriety lives in values far from today's prevailing materialistic and capitalistic aesthetic: it lives long-term, pays attention, uses restraint and mercy. Propriety by definition is the strait gate through which planning has to pass in order not to vanish into its own dream world.[15]

Interpreting his thought, I think the idea that urban planning might be a fact of propriety and not of screamed slogans brings the question back to the fact that for citizens the priority

is not that their city become a world success, but that it might
be a place where daily life favors those who are there living it,
as Benjamin would say, those who conceive urban space as dialectic between the public and the private and democracy as
physicality, as proximity, with all the effects that only proximity
can bring to bear. Obviously, cities are also part of the world
and related to their surroundings and the rest of the world, but
here it is important to point out that it has been forgotten that
they have in the first place to function as laboratories for urban
planning. It was Rebecca Solnit who reminded us in her beautiful *Wanderlust: A History of Walking* that democracy is the possibility of physically circulating in a city (not as beings in vehicles but moving bodies) among other individuals, known and
unknown.[16] The city is the place where meeting each other is an
always-possible event and not subject to risk (as a rule unrelated
to daily life and of one's own volition) and where inhabitants
and passing strangers, established residents and visitors, varied
people and familiar people, can meet one other without fear but
also without apparent purpose. And, as Patrizia Cavalli says in
one of her most beautiful poems, a piazza is an empty place and
whoever wishes may stay there. To put a function onto a piazza
is to kill it. It must remain accessible as a "belonging necessary
to the citizens/to that safe, clear, empty space." As Cavalli says,
the piazza is "an emptiness full of power."[17]

Within this idea of emptiness and of accessibility lies the
guarantee that the society of citizens reproduces its own daily
rules and its own power. This requires that the city be a place
of normal, decorous welcome, modest, if you will, not blaring.
Propriety means the minimum necessary because streets and
sidewalks, open and covered spaces, fountains and trees, footpaths and shops should not cover up with their racket the real
life of the inhabitants, that life made up of the magnificent, tire-
some, entertaining existence and interests tied to every day. In
a recent lecture Franco Berardi took up this concept, talking of
the city as a place of the most forgotten term of the revolutionary

trio: *liberté, egalité, fraternité*. This third element, as opposed to the other two, is not talking about a field of rights, but a field of reciprocal production, the field without which society cannot reproduce itself. Fraternity is not a "value" but a condition. Without it, the city is an empty box that is prey to the slogans.

Milan, Italy

What a strange place. Whoever arrives there from outside and is not used to it is surprised that it is "intentionally" scruffy. As if the most important figure in the line-up on the plain were not the magnificent Cathedral, but the absence of details, the will to communicate "here we don't have time" for beauty. A rich city—obviously also poor—but in which the rich have always preferred the internal to the external and in which luxury must be manifested in the huge billboards advertising high fashion. But obviously that doesn't hold up. At the first whiff of a crisis the billboards show themselves for what they are: just two-dimensional. But for those who discover it on foot, in its corners and on its asphalt and bitumen sidewalks, there remains a mystery: the neglect of its urban propriety, the noninvestment in making the city pleasurable to walk around and to stop in. Up until a short time ago this figure of "negligence" seemed to have been compensated for by the prodigality and the fruits of its creative work. But the city of fashion and design has also become the city of corruption and Italian immoral behavior, and fashion and design, apart from the week dedicated to them, do not overflow beyond their own limits, do not present the city with the care which it needs. It is a schizophrenic situation that "holds" however many still are working on it, but why, in spite of this or maybe because of this, does the abstractness prevail over the physical concreteness of the place?

The big undertakings, a quarter to half implemented, are extraordinary operations: the recovery of the Navigli, the "Piazza Unicredit," the partial renovation of the stations. But what about the ordinary things: the improvement of the subway décor—in a sad state since its start—the maintenance of the avenues and the residential areas? These are really too much alike and are still within the ideology of the bedroom suburbs because here "there's no time for details." Why is it that the most active city in Italy remains also its least interesting, the least invested in a general program of upgrading? Expo 2015 is the umpteenth fair with the umpteenth desired effect for visitor attraction. And the surrounding city? If inspiration were going to be the idea Leonardo had for it, a place of water and people, we are a very long way from the perception of how the minutiae of daily life could improve public space. In this strange situation it seems that the true lovers of the city are those organizing the occupations, because at least they acknowledge the public value of the urban form. It is interesting to understand how Milan lives in its microspaces "notwithstanding" the lack of a general idea. Live in Viale Padova with the Latin Americans, live in Viale Sarpi with the Chinese community and in the popular maze around Viale Tibaldi or the mixed places of Eritreans and Latinos around the Lazzaretto. It is a city of microvillages that do not have, apart from Chinatown, a great past, but an ambitious presence of identity. They are spaces the Milanesi consider "marginal," but the ones that would be the central spaces today are "deadened" like a tooth being readied for a root canal under the hand of the dentist. And if shopping has to be the price of centrality, well, that has fallen off a bit and no one seems to be able to think up anything new right away. Milan seems to be a city that is nostalgic for itself and promises everyone that it will turn back to how it once was, but then makes a superhuman effort to talk itself back to the present. Whoever lives there is searching for a refuge there and for a quality that is still all tied up in reports and potential work, but much less to a liking of the city itself. It is a place of understatement in which the inhabitants are accustomed to being "envied" by visitors in search of the Prada outlet and all of a sudden find themselves in the midst of an immense outlet. A city in which immigration from southern Italy has for fifty years given vigor and color to the foggy mists, and to the drawing rooms where the real decisions are made. But nowadays all that is part of a nostalgia and a memory. If this were the America of the Italians, it would risk becoming Detroit. And it is the place par excellence where the "creative classes" have played their cards and today are most humiliated by a parasitic wealth and are incapable of inventing a future.

NOTES

1   Richard Florida, *The Flight of the Creative Class: The New Global Competition for Talent* (New York: HarperCollins, 2005); Florida, *Cities and the Creative Class* (London: Routledge, 2005).

2   Dave Eggers, *The Circle* (New York: Knopf, 2013).

3   http://www.the guardian.com/commentisfree/2013/dec/30/we-need-to-talk-about-ted.

4   Jamie Peck, "Struggling with the Creative Class," *International Journal of Urban and Regional Research* 29, no. 4 (2005): 740.

5   David Harvey, *The Condition of Postmodernity: An Enquiry into the Origins of Cultural Change* (New York: Blackwell, 1989).

6   Loretta Lees, Tom Slater, and Elvin Wyly, *Gentrification* (London: Routledge, 2008).

7   Ippolita, *"La rete è libera e democratica." Falso!* (Rome-Bari: Laterza, 2014); Carlo Ratti, *Architettura Open Source* (Turin: Einaudi, 2014).

8   Architecture for Humanity, http://www.simstat.com/architecture-for-humanity/.

9   Anthony M. Townsend, *Smart Cities: Big Data, Civic Hackers, and the Quest for New Utopia* (New York: Norton, 2013); Carlo Ratti, *Smart City, Smart Citizen* (Milan: Egen, 2013).

10 Mattteo Pasquinelli, ed., *Gli algoritmi del capitale. Accelerazionismo, macchine della conoscenza e autonomia del comune* (Rome: Ombre Corte, 2014).

11 Appello contro la nuova legge Lupi, September 2014, Rete dei Comitati per la difesa del territorio, http://www.territorialmente.it/2014/09/appello-contro-la-nuova-legge-lupi/.

12 Exception: http://www.inu.it/16765/rassegna.stampa/inu-nella-riforma-urbanistica-lupi-prevale-le-componente-edilizia/.

13 La Lupi II counts on "urban renewal" realizable without any rules, "even in the absence of operational planning or discrepancy from the same prior planning agreement" (Art. 17). Absent from the proposal is any protection for the historical centers as is the fashion nowadays (see the Florentine structural plan). Ilaria Agostini, *L'urbanistica è tossica, Lupi sulla città,* in Il Manifesto," November 9, 2014.

14 Salvatore Settis, "La strana alleanza in salsa verde," *La Repubblica*, June 1, 2013, http://temi.repubblica.it/micromega-online/la-strana-alleanza-in-salsa-verde/.

15 Valerio Paolo Mosco and Roger Scruton, *La bellezza: Ragione ed esperienza estetica* (Milan: Vita e Pensiero, 2013).

16 Rebecca Solnit, *Wanderlust: A History of Walking* (New York: Penguin Books, 2000).

17 Patrizia Cavalli, *Pigre divinita e pigra sorte* (Turin: Einaudi, 2006).

CHAPTER 9

Slums: How to Get the Poor to Pay the Costs of the City

IT IS IMPOSSIBLE TO TEAR ONE'S GAZE AWAY FROM THIS reality. Today the dimension and extent of slums all over the world is so oppressive that it represents most of the response to the need for a roof over one's head. This is the other face, the true one, of the myth of urban prosperity, the myth that unfortunately accompanies the expulsion of millions of small farmers from the countryside (see chapter five). In search of a better life, if not for themselves at least for their children and grandchildren, they are attracted to the big cities as if drawn by a magnet. In Mumbai the arrival of hundreds of families is seen every week. In more fortunate circumstances they are able to take possession of a piece of the sidewalk in Fort, spread out their mats, maybe even pitch a tent, and live like that for months, years, washing themselves in the water that runs in the gutter between the street and the sidewalk and defecating in other gutters a bit farther away. Yet these families live out these new conditions like a dream, as if they have landed in a goldmine, represented by Mumbai, the supreme city where all the wealth of India is concentrated, from the financial operations traffic to the movie industry of Bollywood. The dream is so pervasive that every sacrifice is allowed and every subhuman situation acceptable.[1]

Even the proponents of "urban prosperity" from UN-Habitat know that this situation is explosive:

- The poor make up an increasingly large component of Asia-Pacific developing countries' urban populations; urbanization processes in these countries is leading to increased poverty and deprivation in cities.
- Urban poverty challenges are multidimensional, the most visible and enduring faces of which are the growing slum and squatter settlements linked to insecurity of tenure and inability to access basic services.
- The adverse impacts of climate change have intensified the vulnerability of the urban poor, worsened by their informal legal status, limited access to housing, basic services and social protection.[2]

Perhaps no city today equals Mumbai for the disconcerting and terrible Gotham City spell it exerts. It is not by chance that a great part of contemporary Indian literature is concentrated on it, like Vikram Chandra's *Sacred Games*,[3] an extraordinary panorama of the city as the scenario for the struggle between a policeman and the most powerful gangster, each anchored in his own pathological way to the city on the ocean. The documentary narration of Suketu Mehta's *Maximum City* describes the ruthlessness of the police and of the underworld, but also the absurdity of the nightclub circuit and redistributed wealth being relinquished by Jainists.[4] Mumbai is a vise that squeezes not just the poor but also the middle classes, who are scarcely getting by. Another novel not by chance deals with the story of a middle-class apartment building that is "touched" by the rising value of the neighborhood and is an investment company's object of desire. *Last Man in Tower* by Aravind Adiga tells the terrible story of the last pensioner holding out in a building all the other tenants want to abandon in exchange for a handsome compensation.[5] It is an everyday story, the dream of someone who lives in a slum and imagines that one day it will be his turn to receive a miraculous sum of money in exchange for his hovel. The slums in Mumbai, as everywhere else, along with violence and solidarity, illness and hopefulness, short lives and high infant mortality rates, "produce" an upgrading of immense acreages garnished from the swamps, dumping grounds, jungle, and mud that no one wanted before. It is that added value to living that economists struggle to take into account, but it is such a multiplier that it makes the slums acceptable even to those who see them as a threat. A slum is always a neighborhood that could become potentially desirable. In Mumbai the government and the financial sector have not yet decided to chase away the slum-dwellers—as happened in such an atrocious way in Delhi[6]—because they produce a good amount of revenue for the city. Now every "upgrading" project—each year there are various proposals—implies convincing the real estate market to invest so as to offer shelter to the middle class but also on-site alternatives for the slum-dwellers.

In the meantime, as Arjun Appadurai tells us in *The Future as Cultural Fact*,[7] it is the same inhabitants who are developing "upgrading" practices concentrating on public toilets and running water, which become the subject of actual "toilet festivals." Appadurai points out how these practices are far from a "bird's eye view" vision of the slums; they are tied to a logic of daily mediation which is far removed from a general urban planning theory. It is that logic of "staying," the immanent logic that very often escapes those doing the planning, as well as those working in the NGOs. It is not by chance that the most glamorous plan of the new Indian prime minister (the Muslim-killer), Narendra Modi, actually concentrates on the production of millions of johns for all the Indian people.[8] He who is a past master of populist logic has understood very well how to link a paternalistic approach to a vision which would please the whole world, that of an India where people don't defecate in the streets.

The johns have become the ambiguous symbol on which one bets the "political" and cultural future of the slums. It seems

almost like taking a two-hundred-year leap back and finding the
archeology of the word "slum" in Victorian London. As then,
the political question on which reformers and populists were
appointed was hygiene. Victor Hugo maintained that the sewers
of Paris were the real conscience of the city. Today the slums are
places of filth but they are also the places where it is recycled
and the places where filth becomes the symbol of difference. It
is a debate that for the most part is ideological and political.[9]
In Kenya a nongovernmental organization produced comical
posters with flying WCs, alluding to the use of plastic bags for
defecation with the view of promoting this as a solution to the
lack of sanitary infrastructure in the slums of Nairobi.[10] And
in Caracas the artist Marjetica Potrč, with the help of a local
collective, has constructed "Dry Toilet," a nonflushing toilet
and sewage system that has been exhibited in various museums
in Europe and the United States.[11] For Appadurai the toilet
festivals organized by the inhabitants of Dharavi is a sign of a
changing viewpoint, from abjection to subjectivity.[12]

But there is also the possibility that this type of celebration
reinforces the link between poverty and filthiness, and the moral
hierarchy between the haves and the have-nots of a private form
of hygiene. Thus the Indian middle classes are opposed to the
construction of public toilets in their neighborhoods because,
they say, that is the sign of being a slum.

In an article on urban planning in the barrios of Caracas,
Carlos Brillembourg insists that there is nothing informal in
these new parts of the city.[13] The barrios are not lacking in
form. This must be understood because it challenges the shape
of the colonial city and the disappointing utopias of modern
urban planning. The morphology of the barrios represents
an "antistate." Brillembourg maintains that animism is at the
base of life in the barrios. He links his assertion to the work
of Michael Taussig on commodity fetishism and the cult of
the devil in South America as creative resistance to capitalism. Taussig maintains that this cult of the devil was developed

by Bolivian miners and Colombian workers on the sugarcane plantations as a response to their forced labor for starvation wages.[14] Brillembourg argues that the same cult is found in the barrios for new commodities like skateboards and athletic shoes. Constructing barrios is a type of sorcery in which "the devil is called upon to revenge the injustice of the poor, and human-made filth is considered the medium for this sorcery."[15]

In these controversies there is a mixture of "postcolonial" and "poor studies"—an outrageous expression that is beginning to raise its head in university departments in America and elsewhere. It is a mixture supported by post-Foucault and post-Derrida theories. Homi Bhabha, one of the founders of postcolonial studies, sees in the informal settlements the materialization of the "third space" between the first and third world as liminal space for the creativity of the urban poor.[16]

The *favelas* (shantytowns) are transition spaces and neighborhoods in constant transformation. According to some scholars the space theorized by Deleuze and Guattari, that nomadic and rhizomic space, must be kept in mind.[17] A root can grow in every direction, refusing any notion of a hierarchic order, affirming a patchwork quality and a radical heterogeneity. All these theories! What a heavy responsibility on the shoulders of the residents of those rough-and-ready neighborhoods! And what a small amount of fieldwork there is, how few researchers dive into the always different and seldom predictable reality of those haphazard settlements. In a 2008 interview, Anacláudia Rossbach, a cofounder of Slum/Shack Dwellers International (SDI), which represents a huge movement of informal settlements throughout the world, points out exactly this aspect: "It is important to talk to one another, to exchange experiences, but we must always verify things in place, that is the only way to give credibility to the methodology of involvement."

In her book on the favelas in Rio, Janice Perlman, a North American anthropologist who has studied them while living there over a period of forty years and who founded the

Mega-Cities Project in Rio, gives a panoramic overview of the situation of world habitat.[18]

In Asia, just as in Africa and in Latin America, favelas, *bidonvilles*, slums, *barrios marginales* are ways in which the urban revolution is being confirmed. According to United Nations estimates, today 55 percent of the world's population is urban, and this proportion is projected to reach 68 percent by 2050.[19] Today in Latin America 31 percent of the population are living in slums, in Africa 71 percent (25 percent in the Maghreb), in Asia, 59 percent. In 2000 Rio had a population of six million inhabitants, a million of them in favelas. From 2000 to 2005 this proportion has increased in the favelas, where the population has augmented at a rate five times higher than the rest of the city. The favelas demonstrate the people's capacity for finding themselves a home and for constructing a true and real settlement, but above all for responding to the need for a roof in ways that no public policies of popular housing would ever be able to offer. Moreover, the favelas in Rio are often found in areas with incredible panoramic views, on the steep cliffsides of the *morros* (let's not forget that Rio is a city wrapped in tropical forest, and in the *Mata Atlântica* of which the steep cliffs are a part). But in the face of this capacity there is a difficult situation, often suspended between the danger of forced evictions and the risk of landslides in the rainy season and the struggle between the drug traffickers and the police death squads charged with the cleanup of the favelas themselves in view of the World Cup or the candidacy of Rio as a world city.

Janice Perlman's research in Rio has spanned three generations of *favelados*, so she has seen the birth and death of entire favelas such as Catacumba, and the transformation of others such as Nova Brasilia, Duque de Caxias, but also others better known like Rocinha. And she has witnessed the implementation of different policies, from those that stigmatize the favelas with the expulsion of the inhabitants to those that transform them into objects of international and national projects for improvement and upgrading, up to the myth of the "chic favela" and its horrific counterpoint of the war on drugs within the favelas themselves. The difference between the myth and the reality is in the words of interviews from the seventies up to today (retrieved with patient diligence or else garnered by means of consolidated and long-term friendships and hospitality). In the favelas one lives, one organizes oneself, one creates community and city, but they remain stigmatized places, separated from the rest of the city. Whoever gets out does not return willingly, and between the favelas and the rest of the city there is an enormous social gap. The public policies of President Lula da Silva and his successors often vacillate between the violent intervention of the police and bulldozers and the international appeal that promote social issues like a feather in one's cap. Perlman is clear in refusing any mythologizing of marginality, but she stands up for the decriminalization of the favelados and works assiduously to understand which policies will really improve conditions: for example, property is no longer an important question, while the rights of the its use are, as in the idea of the favela as a "common good." And she is certainly in favor of blending the favelas into the life of the city with courageous and even architectural interventions, like those executed by a great Argentinian architect, Jorge Mario Jáuregui, who believes in physical connections: bridges, streets, cable cars.[20] He is not alone in this belief.

This heritage of forty years of life and fieldwork serves not only in Rio's favelas but in the rest of the worlds constructed by the marginalized, in the slums of Mumbai as well as in the enormous city slums of Lagos. Dismantling the myth, offering analysis of the hard reality helps the operators—architects, planners and administrators—but above all helps the inhabitants to take into account their power of hope linked to a perspective of housing as part of human dignity.

In any case today the debate on the slums is tangled up in a diatribe between those who condemn the use of the word and those who hold that slums are "the solution" to the problem of housing. Postcolonials like Susan Nuttall and Achille Mbembe criticize Michael Watts, who describes slums as the characteristic that defines the development of modern African metropolises and therefore denies them their character as true cities.[21] Vyjayanthi Rao maintains that slums have become a shortcut for a teleology of the dysfunction of the cities in South East Asia.[22] And Tom Angotti accuses Mike Davis of fomenting in his *Planet of Slums* a simplistic duality and ignoring the multiplicity of connections between formal and informal housing.[23] Hernando de Soto, in a neoliberal key, maintains that it is necessary to formalize informal property in order to battle poverty.[24] De Soto is an economist and his idea is that the key to the solution of future urban problems lies in informal settlements. The poor are an extraordinary resource because they perform on their own, produce revenue, and raise the value of land that nobody else wants. Moreover, in the slums and in the favelas there is a creativity that the "normal" city doesn't have.

So one comes to the glorification of the most famous slum of all, Dharavi, in Mumbai: the one in the film *Slumdog Millionaire*. In the flyers of organizations that raise funds for the children of Dharavi is written in capital letters: "Dharavi, the biggest slum in Asia." A lot has been written about Dharavi recently, whether in the newspapers or in novels or reports, but the reality that is emerging is that this "hell on earth" is among the least infernal of the megalopoli. Dharavi is one of the most productive slums in the city, and the numbers are very clear: 700 million euros annual turnover. Certainly the per capita income remains very low, an average of 800 euros per year, and the success of the microentrepreneurs of Dharavi (recyclers of skins and cardboard, and in general the recycling of an immense amount of the city's garbage) doesn't mean that the inhabitants have resolved their problems—infrastructure, sewage systems, ensuring the supply of potable and nonpotable water, hygiene. This does not stop some experts, like Suketu Mehta and Gyan

Prakash,[25] from taking this type of urbanization as an example of copying an "informal city." The density of Dharavi, a certain self-organization, and the fact that tight social control could eliminate almost all crime are taken as the pattern of a phenomenon that would make the "wealth of the poor" jump out as a counter-objection to the state and local policies. And it is in the relatively smaller and newer shanty-cities—for example Rafiq Nagar, a slum in Govandi, where the infant mortality rate is extremely high and the principal occupation of its inhabitants is the gathering of trash—that hunger is worst, relatively speaking. Katherine Boo, in a recent book, *Behind the Beautiful Forevers*, denounces the other side of the industriousness of the inhabitants in the slums of Mumbai: the high price of infant mortality, illnesses, daily violence, and abandonment.[26] The neighborhood in which she lived is not famous like Dharavi.

> I think the main thing is that there's this moment of incredible hope in places like Annawadi and urban spaces across India. The slum I'm writing about is surrounded by five luxury hotels, and the people there do still believe that if they work hard and they just find the key, they're going to be able—if not to get to that hotel—then to at least get out of the slums and at least give their children a better life. I think that that's why, particularly for me, writing the book was essentially an act of hope, because if you can really examine what the obstacles are that keep people stuck in places like Annawadi, where they're daily victims of corruption and brutality, if you can lay that out and throw it down and put your best effort into it, then possibly there will be more of an awareness of what's broken in this society and what needs to be fixed.[27]

Dharavi makes news in papers, but the rest of the slums do not. Dharavi has even become one of the favorite locations for the filmmaking industry of Bollywood, who have studios not far from the slums and go there to shoot scenes of gangsters and misery. Dharavi has become the symbol of the small entrepreneur: artisans, mechanics, pastry makers, potters, and embroiderers live here and are disposed to remain, notwithstanding the government's continued attempts to "clean up" the zone. In a city of twenty million inhabitants, of which some 60 percent is made up of slum dwellers, where apartments in the chic zones can cost 15,000 euros per square meter—and even in the poorer areas they are comparatively expensive—space is like gold. Still, at first sight the most famous slum in the world appears truly like an inferno fitted in among jungle swamps, landfills, and disused railway areas, formed like a dense maze of tin and cardboard shacks up to three stories high, mired in dust and immersed in deafening noise. We're talking about three square meters in an excellent location, between the two main railway lines, close to the airport and to the Bandra Kurla Complex, the financial and commercial heart of the city. The population density in this area is around three hundred thousand people per square kilometer, among the highest in the world.

One suspects that the slums are coming into the limelight because a new business is growing up around them, one that sees in the poor the solutions to the problems of the city. The poor are a resource for the rich, and dealing with them is an enormous new field that goes from "poverty studies" programs in the universities, to the businesses of "slum improvement," to a new urban planning that makes poverty a key object of all its new projects. It's fitting that urban renewal is updating itself in this sense, much less so is the calculation to offload the horrific costs of urban pollution, of crowd density, or the inability to handle urban waste. It is not by chance that in a video by Al Jazeera devoted to the slums throughout the world this is a constant. Many inhabitants of these places are truly interested in "filth" in the sense that their survival is linked to searching through city garbage for what is resalable or can even be eaten.

A really beautiful documentary, *Denok and Gareng*, filmed by the Indonesian director Dwi Sujanti Nugraheni in a little "favela" in the jungle surrounding Jogjakarta, tells about a young couple, Denok and Gareng. More precisely, it is about the extended family with whom they live: mother, brothers and sisters, children. The family lives by working in the garbage dumps to find items to sell and to feed the pigs (it is a Muslim family and is marginalized even in this, raising *haram* [unclean] animals to sell them). The gathering and winnowing of the refuse is a complicated activity, because it involves sorting out recoverable foodstuffs for the pigs and the other types of recyclable trash. A tough job, but the documentary shows us the humor, the constant comments on their own poverty and their own misfortune, the strong realization of being on the edge of survival, but also the tenacity, all without rhetoric. The documentary is important because it perfectly portrays the "problem" of the slums, that of being a tool for seeking a means of existence using the city and its garbage as its primary resource. In the long run even the materials that make up the slum itself originate from the city: flattened-out cans, cardboard boxes, tents.

The poor are to the city something to be hidden but who are an essential part life there. The poor and their settlements are the carpet under which the city sweeps what they are incapable of managing, whether it be the recycling of refuse, prostitution, crime, or drug trafficking. Not because these are necessarily features of a slum, but in the "offside" of the informal settlement cities, are concentrated the informality and inequality that serve them so they can continue to grow. On the bodies of the poor, on their lungs and the lungs of their children, on resistance and on the debilitation of illnesses, an economy of poverty is constructed that makes the great urban agglomerations an expansionist fabrication. Urbanization is charging the poor and making a good business from them, and this is the fabrication that must be resisted. Knowing this, it is not easy to make distinctions. Often it is important that there be rights for the inhabitants of the slums and often de Soto could be correct: there is an issue linked to the formalization of informality. And the improvement projects are also important, even if the public sector rarely succeeds in offering such immense solutions.

Only in cities like Singapore with a centralized and very interventionist administration have the slums been eradicated through a public policy of popular housing for everyone. It happened when the island, which has a limited surface and five million inhabitants, was devastated by a fire in the sixties that burned the slum that occupied part of the island and endangered the entire settlement. It is an interesting case, anyway, because it shows how the interest of one city should be conceived as a whole. Slums can be an interim solution, but in the end they are only a commodity for administrators who are unable to offer alternatives and see in the poor who are keeping themselves busy an excellent occasion for unloading their own responsibilities. Singapore is a limited case, because it is a city with a very strong sense of "carrying capacity," but it is valuable as an example of the duty of conceiving the city as a whole and not a collection of parts. But the nullifying point of the urban policies in this field is in defeating the ideology of poverty studies behind which they are hiding. The slums are a manifestation of something much larger. DIY is a widespread practice even for the middle classes, as the story of *gecekondu* of Istanbul tells us,[28] districts where the petty bourgeoisie were rebuilding the city in the manner of their regions of origin. And one of the first measures taken by Erdoğan was the almost total destruction of it all, substituting "his" tower block housing, that was built by "his" real estate constructors.

The problem with poverty studies and their idiocy lies in their having "slummified" processes which are much more extensive than those related to poverty and to emergency. As a good number of indigent people know, there is a "right to build" one's own dwelling that goes beyond emergency considerations and instead responds to an expression of their own identity. Those who are somewhat concerned with vernacular architecture would have to know a bit about it, but above all

so would those who live among indigent populations.[29] Do-it-
yourself, that is, the activity of defining one's own dwelling, is
embraced by increasingly large swaths of the world's population.
All of them are poor, but they are not defined only by poverty.

In 1980 a conference on DIY was organized in Rimini.[30]
John Turner, who had worked for years in the *barrios marginales*
in Lima and had shifted public opinion and the world of
architecture with regard to the enormous phenomenon of DIY,
was there. He fought for acceptance of the principle of autonomy
and the right to housing. Ivan Illich spoke at the conference, as
did Giancarlo De Carlo and Carlo Doglio, and Renzo Piano
participated with his Otranto project. But most important was
the attendance of overseas and Italian DIY protagonists. Thus
the focus was not on the slum or the favela, but the generalized
right to respond to the question of housing in the first person,
without the mediation of a class of professional experts. Today
we return to that debate, arguing that the idea that DIY concerns
only the poor and marginalized masses of Third World countries
is a colonialist idea.

Ragusa Ibla, Italy

*Why Ragusa, that little commune that is the capital of a province in
southeast Sicily? It has fewer than three hundred thousand inhabitants and doesn't sparkle with vivacity, such as being the setting
for nightlife, festivals, or scandals. It is a tranquil city, cradled in a
superb manner between two hilly promontories and across from an
extraordinary landscape of deep valleys and overlooking plateaus.
Partly reconstructed after a terrible earthquake in 1693 that devastated the Val di Noto, it is an example of popular baroque with
stairways and streets that go up and down, underground passages,
observation points over the abyss and high-flying churches and mon-
asteries. A city, anyway, with all the urbanity of a city, and that's why
I want to talk about it. Because urbanity has nothing to do with the
dimension of an inhabited center, but rather with its ambition. It's
urbane to have tree-lined avenues. It's urbane to have people who feel*

obliged to dress to the nines to walk up and down the main street from end to end in the evening. It's urbane to have a rapport between the houses and the streets, that dialogue that integrates places for sitting outside one's homes, with plants and canopies. It's urbane that there is a whole that holds, a forma urbis for which the roofs are appealing and taper toward each other. And urbane is the rapport between the old and the new, between Ragusa Ibla and Ragusa Alta, that awareness of a pleasant difference, a passage between one world and another. The granita ices, coffees in the piazza, and the fellows walking around chatting are urbane. So are the kiosks in the evening as one goes from new Ragusa to old Ragusa, those kiosks that look into the abyss and let you sit and drink an almond milk and gossip about nothing with neighbors.

NOTES

1 Franco La Cecla, *Indian Kiss* (Milan: O Barra O Edizioni, 2011).

2 UN-Habitat, "Addressing Urban Poverty, Inequality, and Vulnerability in a Warming World," *Asia Pacific Issue Brief Series on Urbanization and Climate Change*, no. 1 (2014), http:// http://www.fukuoka.unhabitat.org/programmes/ccci/pdf/1_Addressing_Urban_Poverty_Inequality_and_Vulnerability_in_a_Warming_World.pdf.

3 Vikram Chandra, *Sacred Games* (New York: HarperCollins, 2007).

4 Suketu Mehta, *Maximum City* (New York: Random House, 2005).

5 Aravind Adiga, *Last Man in Tower* (London: Atlantic Books, 2011).

6 Gautam Bhan, "'This Is No Longer the City I Once Knew': Evictions, the Urban Poor and the Right to the City in Millennial Delhi," *Environment and Urbanization* 21, no. 1 (April 2009): 127–42.

7 Arjun Appadurai, *The Future as Cultural Fact: Essays on the Global Condition* (Newcastle: Cambridge Scholars Publishing 2013).

8 Nitya Jacob, "Chain Reaction: India Needs Hygiene Education as Well as New Toilets," *Guardian*, October 8, 2014, https://www.theguardian.com/global-development/poverty-matters/2014/oct/08/india-narendra-modi-toilets-education-hygiene.

9 Ann Varley, "Postcolonializing Informality?," *Environment and Planning D: Society and Space* 31, no. 1 (2013): 1–4.

10 John Gendall, "Co-designing Productive Parks with the Poorest of Kibera, Kenya," *Harvard Design Magazine*, no. 28 (2008): 67–69.

11 Marjetica Potrč and Liyat Esakov, "Growing House, Growing City, in Alfredo Brillembourg, Kristen Feiriss, and Hubert Klumpner, eds., *Informal City: Caracas Case* (Munich: Prestel, 2005), 176–86.

12 Appadurai, *The Future as Cultural Fact.*

13 Carlos Brillembourg, "The New Slum Urbanism of Caracas, Invasions and Settlements, Colonialism, Democracy, Capitalism and Devil Worship," *Architectural Design* 74, no. 2 (2004): 77–81.

14 Michael Taussig, *The Devil and Commodity Fetishism in South America* (Chapel Hill: University of North Carolina Press, 1980).

15 Brillembourg, "The New Slum Urbanism of Caracas," 81.

16 Homi Bhabha, The *Location of Culture* (London: Routledge, 1994).

17 Gilles Deleuze and Félix Guattari, *Millepiani: Capitalismo e Schizofrenia*, 3rd ed. (Milan: Castelvecchi, 2010).

18 Janice Perlman, *Favela: Four Decades of Living on the Edge in Rio de Janeiro* (Oxford: Oxford University Press, 2010), 41–61.

19 United Nations, *World Urbanization Prospects 2018*, https://population.un.org/wup/.

20 Jorge Mario Jáuregui, *Estrategias de articulacion urbana: Proyecta y gestion de asentamientos perifericos en America Latina: Un enfoque transdisciplinario* (Buenos Aires: Ediciones Fado, Universidad de Buenos Aires, 2003); Jorge Mario Jáuregui, "Urban and Social Articulation: Megacities, Exclusion and Urbanity," in Felipe Hernandez, Peter Kellett, and Lea K. Allen, eds., *Rethinking the Informal City: Critical Perspectives from Latin America* (New York: Berghahn, 2010), 207–23; Elizabeth Mossop, "Extreme Urbanism: The Importance of Complexity," in *The Favela-Bairro Project: Jorge Mario Jauregui Architects*, ed. Rodolfo Machado (Cambridge, MA: Harvard University Press, 2005), 61–77.

21 Sarah Nuttal and Achille Mbembe, "A Blasé Attitude: A Response to Michael Watts," *Public Culture* 17, no. 1 (Winter 2005): 193–201; Michael Watts, "Baudelaire over Berea, Simmel over Sandton?," *Public Culture* 17:1, 181–92.

22 Vyjayanth Rao, "Slum as Theory, the South/Asian City and Globalization," *International Journal of Urban and Regional Research* 30, no. 1 (2006): 225–32.

23 Tom Angotti, "Apocalyptic Anti-urbanism: Mike Davis and His Planet of Slums," *International Journal of Urban and Regional Research* 30, no. 4 (2006): 96–97.

24 Hernando de Soto, *The Mystery of Capital: Why Capitalism Triumphs in the West and Fails Everywhere Else* (London: Bantam, 2000); see also Ahmed M. Soliman, *A Possible Way Out: Formalizing Housing Informality in Egyptian Cities* (Lanham, MD: University Press of America, 2004).

25 Suketu Mehta, "Looking for the Bird of God," in Ricky Burdett and Dayan Sudjic, *Living in the Endless City* (London: Phaidon, 2011); Gyan Prakash, *La città color zafferano: Bombay tra metropoli e mito* (Milan: Bruno Mondadori, 2012).

26 Katherine Boo, *Behind the Beautiful Forevers: Life, Death, and Hope in a Mumbai Undercity* (New York: Random House, 2012).

27 Chiki Sarkar, "A Conversation with Katherine Boo and Aman Sethi," *Brick: A Literary Journal*, no. 89 (Summer 2012), https://brickmag.com/a-conversation-with-katherine-boo-and-aman-sethi/.

28 Aylin B. Yildirim, *Informal Istanbul: Potential of the Gecekondu and Alternatives to Redevelopment in the Case of Karanfilkoy* (Cambridge, MA: Harvard University, 2006), available at http://www.fflch.usp.br/centro dametropole/ISA2009/assets/papers/01-A-8.pdf; Orhan Esen, "Istanbul's Gecekondus," LSE Cities, 2009, https://lsecities.net/media/objects/articles/istanbuls-gecekondus/en-gb/.

29 Paul Oliver, ed., *Encyclopedia of Vernacular Architecture of the World* (Cambridge: Cambridge University Press, 1997).

30 CABAU R&A (Renzo Agostini et al.), *Il potere di abitare* (Florence: Libreria Editrice Fiorentina, 1981).

CHAPTER 10

Urbanicide and Street Food

CITIES GOOD FOR EATING, CITIES GOOD FOR THINKING—
one could paraphrase Lévi-Strauss's insight about what is edible
or not.[1] For him, only that which fits into a system of thought,
wild or not, is comestible.

For cities the opposite is true. Their desirability as a visible
offering of daily food allows those who visit them or who live in
them to think of them as humanly habitable. There is an urban
dimension in the alimentary attraction that is so extremely pervasive and powerful that its absence is immediately obvious.
Cities obsessed with regulations and hygiene and police super-
vision lose whatever desirability they might have had. Neutral
and insipid cities drag the stroller past aseptic windows, con-
ducting one to high-backed chairs and scrupulously clean tables,
to consume the packaged food accurately cleaned of all attributes that might possibly cause a shock to the palate, the olfactory
system, or the stomach. When this is happening you can be sure
that this city does not offer much attraction to those who were
born there. Urbanity (and not urban planning) consists in an
olfactory and visible dimension, tactile and resonant with the
confusion of street markets that have everything to contribute.

Woe to the cities that destroy their own street markets in
order to become *world cities*. And they do it, too: it's happening
right under our very eyes with the encouragement and cover
of international organizations such as UNESCO. All done and

commissioned for the protection of the cultural patrimony.[2]
The food markets, the street food stands with their smoke and
smells, with their clutter and their rubbish, are seen as disrup-
tive to the tourist aspect of the city. Magnificent and lively
Latin American cities are being menaced to death by those who
believe that a city should be a picture postcard for tourists and
not a vital living organism.[3] This approach, which is not much
discussed by the archistars and the urban planners, rests on the
basis of a terrifying ignorance of how "cities are made," of what
constitutes them. Food: street markets where they sell fruit and
vegetables, fish and meat, bread and wine, maize and bamboo,
tofu and shellfish, or where they sell all these things cooked,
fried, boiled, smoked for regular customers who seat themselves
beside and in the market itself: all this is what has always been
the source from which the city springs up and develops.

There are cities like Lisbon in which even the poorest little
old ladies don't hesitate to eat street food, and this causes strong
price fixing for the cost of a meal: it costs less to eat seated at
a little table in the shade next to the blue tiles than to make
something at home. Barcelona, in spite of the tourist hordes,
is just as good, and the markets such as La Boqueria, once
invaded only by German swarms, is now the domain of the
local inhabitants. Eating means eating in the open spaces of the
public squares, in the cool shade of the alleyways, under the
slants of the stairways, in the hidden halls where they sell *turrón*,
and where you can drink *horchata de chufa*.

A city consists of its public celebrations of food. These
make the spaces and delineate their boundaries, rendering a
square or an open space, a corner or an alley into something
that creates opportunities for its surrounding space. Markets
do it even more, be they weekly or daily, out in the open, in
the souks or in the side streets or under the cover of metal or
wooden roofs. The quarters are congregated around the markets,
which influence the other enterprises, merchandise, assets, cafes,
artists, idlers, and auctioneers. The markets form the layout of a

good part of the cities that we know, even when they have been repudiated and dismissed as a sign of backwardness.

In Selatan, an enormous island south of Sulawesi, the markets delineate the areas between the sea and the built-up villages, where huge spreads of cloves are laid out to dry in the equatorial sunshine. The spice markets in tortured Damascus and in tortured Aleppo, as well as in Istanbul, Jogjakarta, and Penang, help us get a notion of what a space would be like without an odor. The aroma of the spices pervades and identifies entire blocks, underpinning them, making them exciting and at times almost unbearable. Like those streets in Mexico that are lined with all the varieties of chiles and garlic and every imaginable type of pepper.

There are cities one can recognize with one's eyes closed because of their aromas. My Palermo (these days mostly garbage) up to a few years ago was recognizable from the whiff of sugar that came from the pastry makers' workshops. There are cities that make themselves known through the smell of bread. Baking time is the moment when the night becomes fit to live in as its fragrance wafts out over humans who are showing no signs of waking up.

A good part of these architectures has no need of walls, or columns, or arches, or roofs. They are ephemeral structures that can provide enough to let the passersby be struck by the color and variety, the light and the crazy piles of fruit, of the silvery flash of fish and the pungent smell of the meats and the processed vegetables. The stalls, the tents, the crates all get hidden by the piles of olives, snails, melons, eggplants, Alphonso mangoes. Who buys and who sits around matters little when it comes to the decor of the benches or the tables. The substance is what comes smoking to the tables. But the architecture of street markets is never accidental. Their merchandise is phantasmagorical, making a circus for sight, smell, and hearing.

The market is the out and out place for the artistic performance of food. The sellers construct pyramids of vegetables and melons, ziggurats of nuts and artichokes, and they sing to you, embrace you, and dance about with gestures to entice passersby. Watch the doughnut and candy sellers in China, while they twirl the dough, singing as they form the shapes. Watch the performance of Nino "*u ballerino*" as he prepares the spleen sandwiches in the Olivuzza district in Palermo, admire his automatic and obsessive gestures, as he transforms himself into a food-producing machine. Or in Istanbul marvel in the Kurdish and Romani communities of Tarlabasi, where the fruit vendors harmonize their songs with the rhythm of the scales. When one is selling in the streets, synesthesis is the name of the game: mixing aromas with the "spiels." In Sicily, Andalusia, and Latin America those "patter songs," the shout-outs made with a throaty voice, have their roots in the *cante jondo* of flamenco and *duende* reminiscent of Lorca.

Food is an artistic regime, but above all it is a moral regime. It makes up daily routine and strengthens human relations with an aesthetic that becomes a habit, an ethic, the shared rules. Taste is not an anarchic assessment of flavors, aromas, and visions. It is the sharing of a judgment system that becomes the daily mood, the temperament which gives a sense of community and harmony to life.

Street food provides an aesthetic and tasty virtuosity. There are streets in Bangkok where those in the know come, people who know that here is the place one eats well, not in any restaurant. There are soups at the corners of Sukhumvit that seem to be made from nothing, *acqua cotta* (cooked water), and when you taste them they make you envision a lightly salted concoction of faintly bitter galangal with a final hint of ginger. And you are seated on the only chair at the tiny table right in front of the stove where the soup is prepared.

In Penang or Kuala Lumpur, the entire Chinatown is a paean to street food, with plastic chairs and paper cups.

In Beijing or Shanghai, they line up to buy toasted nuts, yogurt, skewers, wontons of all types, and you get it that there

are no set hours for eating. The Chinese eat all the time and everywhere. In the morning they have breakfast standing in front
of enormous pots of dumplings, which are cooked by being
switched around with amazing skill on a single burner. For the
Chinese the city is a hotbed of food, and the night markets are
a challenge to the daily markets.

In Fukuoka, on the Japanese island of Kyushu, in the middle-class modern neighborhoods, the people come out to the
sidewalks to eat in the little huts on wheels that turn into sushi
bars, tempura and ramen bars, and places where one eats and
drinks deep into the night sheltered by curtains with the special-
ties written on them.

Street food is also the first true manifestation of the connection between goods and publicity. In Palermo, the sellers
of *stigghiola*, veal offal on the grill, identify their food trucks
with high clouds of smoke. They are the results of the sizzling
fat that fills the air with the irresistible aroma of the innards.
Cooked over a flame, sautéed in a wok, stirred in deep cauldrons,
the spectacle of food preparation is in itself a performance that
attracts the passersby. One stops to watch, one comments on
the cook's skill, one wonders what hidden ingredients are added
in. For all that, the street markets seem so modern, and they
invented public relations techniques long before the first ads
appeared on Morris columns and on the walls of Paris.

Together with the art of calling out the wares, the other
component of the markets is the placement of food as the
direct relationship between those who cook and those who eat.
There's no intercession of menu, ordering, and servers. The eater
is a direct and severe critic of the cook, and it's because of this
that street food is particularly good: it's always under constant
and direct control.

There are entire areas of Tokyo where one stoops down to
get into a cabin that hosts no more than six or seven regulars.
These are right in the center of the city, in Shinjuku, in an alley
called "of the drunks." Here one waits, drinking saké or shocho,

potato alcohol, while the proprietor cooks what you are about to eat right before your very eyes. The spectacle of the cooking, of the frying, and the "salto," the stirring, the spectacle of kneading, of arranging on the plate, are the daily routine that make it possible to transform the rhythms of the day into rituals and turns places into temples of citizenship.

The Greeks knew that symposia were an institution of democracy on a par with the agora. To understand how the others among whom you find yourself living "really" are, and to get the hang of the city, you have to watch them as they eat and drink and see how they handle food and drink. Wine is not an invention of the person who despondently inaugurated the happy hour. It is rather the first proof of cohesion of citizens among themselves. It is not an aperitif, it's the cement of sociability.

All this is threatened by the stupidity of current urban planning, by the ignorance of those who believe that a "creative city" is the result of studying architecture and nothing to do with what one "normally" finds in the street. The creativity of food in cities is the matrix of every other form of creativity, because it is a diffuse mixture of voices, visions, lights, movements, packed down and spread out with perspective.

We need to do our best right now to defend and save the street markets. More than every market for locally produced items, more than every organic market, it is the street markets that ensure that Mother Earth is represented. Because these markets are preeminently the setting for organic and cultural variety. If they are driven from the city centers, if they are transformed into "picnic areas," they will lose the multifunctionality that makes them the matrix of urbanity. We don't go to the markets just to eat but also to walk around, observe, comment, meet one another. The architects and the planners and UNESCO are convinced that it is a question of "folklore" to preserve, whereas what is on the line is the innate vitality of a place, its habitability. Food is not "folklore," it is a cultural system with an extraordinary capacity for self-innovation. It is an autopoietic structure which generates and regenerates itself, as long as its ease and indeterminacy are respected. Transforming a street market into a shopping center is like believing that rock is an app that can be downloaded onto your cell phone.

There is a reality to which even those who battle for healthy, fair-trade, and locally produced food, are blind. It is that this food has need of a specific place that is not the intelligent Whole Foods or Eataly, but above all the little local market or the street overrun by those who cook the food right in front of us. The European Community is the prime enemy of all that, who with their rules and regulations want to transform catering into something clinical and food into medicine. There is a dimension to food that is "dirty," fatty, fried, oily, with aromas that only an expert can appreciate, which forms part of the great regional cultures. From Florentine tripe sandwiches, to the offal skewers in Puglia or Sicily, to rotten bamboo, to tofu "pourri." A lot of food can be "difficult," including the magnificently aromatic durian fruit, which would never make it past the European hygiene commission. This is total madness, because it eliminates from the food system the extremes that are essential for its survival. And it transforms the competence of the consumer into the expectation of a patient in a hospital waiting room.

Moreover, and this is essential for those who claim they are battling for fair-trade food, it is the food markets and the stands where food is cooked in the streets that set prices and make nutrition affordable to the poorest and the homeless. Make the rounds of the markets in Mumbai or Allahabad and you will understand what it means: that the poor can feed themselves with an abundant overflow which only the street merchants can provide, by being able to use up what is not eaten at the end of the day by redistributing it.

Street food, street vendors, and street markets are the most powerful reserves of the economy: not only do they keep prices lower, but they also create jobs around themselves, porters, distributors, cleaners, and above all are a direct channel for farmers and small producers. They are that city/country connection that, if ignored, shatters realities for both of them. The countrysides are essential for the survival of the cities, and their "figurative" presence is expressed in the street markets. The street vendors are a guarantee of safety in entire parts of the city, with a vivacity and urbanity that could never be reproduced in a shopping center. I was wandering around with students from ITU, the state Faculty of Architecture of Istanbul, through the bazaars of the city and then through the new shopping centers. They were astonished that they had never realized the richness which only informality can provide as opposed to the "frigidity" of the shop windows. Street food and street markets are a mixture of construction, usage, and management of urban space.

For some years there has existed a dense network of organizations and individuals tied to the informal sector. In 2014 in Rome a big meeting of street vendors was organized, something less fashionable than slow food, but more efficacious. Cities put together a very important document: *The Urban Informal Workforce: Street Vendors.*[4] I am summarizing the conclusions here—the research was conducted "in the field" of the street markets in Accra in Ghana, Ahmedabad in India, Durban in South Africa, Lima in Peru, and Nakuru in Kenya.

The sale of food in the streets is an important source of employment in many cities: in sub-Saharan Africa it accounts for 24 percent of the total informal sector, in India for 14 percent, and in Latin America for 9 percent.

Fifty percent of the street vendors obtain their supplies from informal providers, and this rises to 77 percent in the case of fruit and vegetable supplies.

Three sellers out of four pay for a license for the use of their patch of ground, and the same proportion pay for light, electricity, and water. Half of them pay for the use of a toilet, and four out of ten pay for parking space.

In the face of this, they are often in a situation of insecurity and of moral and physical abuse, due to the behavior of the police and the municipal guards, demands of "protection money" from racketeers, and of the administrations themselves when they decide to clear out the street markets and chase out the vendors. The situation is even worse in the case of women vendors.

Some of the recommendations the document made for the policymakers are:

> Urban planning and local economic development strategies should explicitly recognize street vendors as workers for the role they play in generating economic activity, providing jobs, and bringing retail goods to consumers. . . . It is important to recognize the need to accommodate street vendors in public space rather than (or in addition to) attempting to relocate vendors into off-street commercial spaces. While relocation may be possible for some vendors, particularly those who are employers and operate several street stalls simultaneously, many are unable to accumulate enough capital to invest in an off-street stall or to generate regular and sufficient earnings to support monthly rent payments. . . . In addition, planning authorities should consider ways of designing and delivering urban infrastructure to support productivity in the informal economy.[5]

We have to remember that this organization operates in conjunction with the International Labor Organization (ILO)[6] and that their recommendations are not biased but reflect a rationalization of the true well-being and economy of a region. The informal sector is not a "marginal" or illegal sector of the economy (even though illegality often gets factored into that sector). It is simply a sector of which it is hard to take a census and that is based on the initiative of individuals or of single families. It is a branch of the economy that borders on subsistence, like domestic work and the network of local connections, but often produces more than the "real" economy. The Hanoi police are well aware of this: they earn less than a woman selling *pho* in the marketplace.[7] Eliminating the informal economy would mean throwing entire nations on the rocks, but above all, and this is what interests us here, it would destroy the productive and autopoietic capacity, the social reproductivity of a city. Up to now no one has understood this—the mummification of cities through the work of prigs and an ignorant system of urban planning that provokes as many urbanicides and UNESCOcides.

Minsk, Belarus

The strangest thing about Minsk is the Russian tourists who come there because they are in a nostalgic crisis for the time of the Soviet Union. A nostalgia shared by director Valery Todorovsky, who came there to shoot Stilyagi, *a musical set in the fifties about young rockabilly Muscovites who dressed like their American contemporaries and played and listened to jazz. Only in Minsk is one able to recreate a corner of Russia behind the iron curtain without too many problems, without the invasive presence of neon signs, billboards, and supersized plasma screens. In effect, Minsk, with a million and a half inhabitants, the capital of Belarus, governed for the past ten years by a local dictator, Lukashenko, is very similar to the world before the fall of the Wall. Its wide avenues are bordered with monumental Soviet-style buildings, it has big parks, statues of Lenin and even of the evil Feliks Dzerzhinsky, founder of the Cheka, predecessor of the KGB, and it brings to mind a past that has not passed. But then you remember that this is not an iron curtain, but one made of tin. You can go shopping for European and Western products, there's internet, there's Facebook, and above all, the people are not those from a place of regimentation. Many of the people are young, many of them are women, beautiful, with those long Slavic legs, which they show to perfection on the highest heels. I asked Francesco Cataluccio, author of the best guidebook to the Eastern countries,* Vado a vedere se di là è meglio *(Sellerio Publishers), what I could expect from Minsk, and he told me that the most beautiful women in the world are there, but they often have mustaches. I imagined that it was badmouthing passed on to him by Kapuscinski, who was born in Belarus, but being a good Pole, he detested it with all his heart (in* Imperium *he says it is the only place where he felt really frightened). Here there are many more women than men, perhaps as a result of the war, during which there were massacres and the total slaughter of the Jews, who made up a good half of the population. There is a beautiful book by Ludmila Ulitskaya* (Daniel Stein, Interpreter) *that tells the story of Oswald Rufeisen, an adolescent Jew who saved the lives of six hundred of the thousands of Jews imprisoned in Mir Castle in the south of Belarus and destined to be annihilated by the Gestapo. That whole ancient world of the* shtetl, *the Jewish villages whose life and culture was so bound up in that region—the life depicted in the paintings of Chagall, himself a Jew and born here—all wiped out. Oswald Rufeisen was able to organize a flight and a resistance in the thick forests of spruce and birches.*

Today in Belarus one inhales a sense of hiatus between now and the preceding story. This region has paid heavily for being a zone of passage, from Napoleon to Hitler to Stalin. But it is also possible that the demographic imbalance could be due to the proximity of Chernobyl, because of the medicinal doses of hormones with which the inhabitants of Minsk were stuffed and which could have altered "in a female way" the demographic equilibrium. Certainly one has also to consider the alcohol consumption of the males, here as in Russia, and the high mortality rate it causes among young men. Anyway, it is a pleasure to walk around the city, there is an orderliness, an almost Scandinavian cleanliness, and then there is a strange kind of undertone, a relative lack of advertising. What is surprising is the lack of images of the dictator. It seems he is aware of not being very beloved, he who is considered an outsider of peasant extraction, who barely speaks Belarus . . . Very few billboards, very few posters, to the point that it is hard to work out from outside what types of merchandise is being offered for sale in the shops. You approach a monumental glass door in the center and find yourself in a modest little local bakery. You open what looks like a door to an apartment building and find instead an immense pharmacy or a giant clothing store. The impression for us is that we are in a place that is not obsessed with marketing, but when you delve into the matter you don't turn up a political motive, but a coupon for 20 percent off on all the merchandise that comes into Belarus, and that amount goes directly into the safe of Lukashenko. There's not much left over for publicity. This lofty and protectionist political move, however, is more ideological than real. Belarus has refused to pay Putin for the gas that comes to them from Russia, but recently Lukashenko has changed his mind and says that he will pay up. The tug of war is with the neighbors (Belarus refused to rejoin the Russian Federation), and with Europe it has a somewhat anti-American function.

Deep down, they are open to everyone who wants to invest here, Turkey most of all. The general effect is of a "Baltic" country, a tranquil population, a pleasant city, and above all a magnet for those from the West in search of sexual adventures. But even here this is a bit in question. The beautiful women of Minsk are not pushovers who are going to give themselves to whoever promises to marry them and take them away or simply make them munificent companions. They are independent women, with a salary, however modest, earned since they were quite young, they travel—even with economic difficulties—they go abroad to study and speak languages but in the end they want to return and settle down here. One of the most exhilarating scenes you can see takes place at the crossing of Prospekt Nezalezhnosti, "Independence Avenue," the main thoroughfare that cuts across Minsk, in front of McDonald's. Here is where the Italians meet to hook up, bronzed from the tanning studios, gold chains around their necks, with their names on them, Nino, Salo, Pino, and a desire to move fast because they have a plane to catch in a couple of days. The twentysomething blondes pass by, but they are the ones who do the approaching, with open-minded boldness and with an air of knowing only too well who's doing what and to whom. We're in a simulation of an Eastern country and the simulation is being acted out more by the feminine gender than by the masculine strangers. The women here have a strength based on the harshness of the past, on a history of female independence, on a work ethic to which they have become habituated by the tradition of masculinity distracted by alcohol and politics. Perhaps also because of this the male strangers somehow win their attention. And the flow of men in search of companions and wives continues, the Turks in the lead, and in the evenings the playacting goes merrily on in the discos and the local hangouts. The real problem with this country is its relatively youthful identity. There's not much literature, little music, almost no local culture. The monumental elegance and the serenity of the tree-lined avenues and the workers' quarters give the whole place a kind of virginal air, of something that has yet to begin yet is at the same time engulfed in melancholy. Here is a sort of tabula rasa, a lack of the strong signs that give place to a respectable world, understated, a modesty that, unfortunately, comes not by choice.

NOTES

1   Claude Lévi-Strauss, *The Raw and the Cooked* (New York: Harper and Row, 1969).

2   An example of this is the history of the churches of Lalibela in Ethiopia. Scarcely had they been designated as a UNESCO World Heritage sites when the local church authorities demolished everything that was around them, in other words a magnificent collection of vernacular architecture. Obviously, UNESCO cannot be held responsible for either the absolute ignorance of those affected by their proclamation. Could be that they still haven't understood and that they could invent a manner of defending the urbanistic and social context where the monuments are located?

3   Marco d'Eramo, "UNESCOcide," *New Left Review*, no. 88 (July–August 2014): 47–53.

4   Sally Roever, *Informal Economy Monitoring Study Sector Report: Street Vendors*, Inclusive Cities, April 2014, https://https://www.wiego.org/ sites/default/files/migrated/publications/files/IEMS-Sector-Full-Report-Street-Vendors.pdf; see also Roever, "Informal Economic Sector Livelihood Profile: Street Vendors," in *AAPS Planning Education Toolkit: The Informal Economy*, Appendix A, 2011, Inclusive Cities, http://www.inclusivecities. org/wp-content/uploads/2012/07/InformalEconomyToolkit_sectorpro-files.pdf. I owe this information to Costanza La Mantia and to her work in

South Africa on the informal economies and town planning. Costanza La Mantia, "Humanizing Urbanism: On Embracing Informality and the Future of Johannesburg," in *Sustainable Urban Development and Globalization*, eds. Agostino Petrillo and Paola Bellaviti (Cham: Springer, 2018), 49–63; La Mantia, "Città dei Morti nella post-rivoluzione. Politiche urbane e nuove sfide socio-culturali al Cairo," *Territorio* 61, no. 2 (2012): 98–103.

5   Roever, *Informal Economy Monitoring Study Sector Report: Street Vendors*, 61.

6   ILO and WIEGO, *Women and Men in the Informal Economy: A Statistical Picture* (Geneva: International Labour Office, 2013).

7   Franco La Cecla, *Good Morning Karaoke* (Milan: TEA, 2004).

CHAPTER 11

Paris as Province in the XXII Century

WHY PROVINCE? BECAUSE THIS CITY, WHICH HAS ALWAYS looked down at the cities around it—and still does—is living today with the anguish of being considered marginal on a global level. And to give itself tone it is tacitly and slowly aligning itself with the most fashionable trends in European urban space: it is haphazardly attempting to become an orderly and regulated city in which every wrinkle caused by life in the streets and the crowd in the streets is completely smoothed away. The capital so dear to Walter Benjamin is becoming provincially normal, a "disciplinary" space that does not allow any sort of unexpectedness and submissively obeys globalizing rhetoric. That it succeeds is a different kettle of fish precisely because in this attempt Paris is far from being a leader but is instead a simple and confused participant in a situation guided from elsewhere.

I lived with Piero Zanini in Paris in the last twenty years with joy, rage, boredom, and annoyance. Piero is a shrewd observer and an indefatigable walker, and with him I have learned to understand the little changes and slight displacements as the city is mutating. We both have lived in the most "unpopular" part of Paris, between Barbes, la Goutte d'Or, and Chateau Rouge,[1] which for over a century has been a quarter for the working class and immigrants. Over time it has hosted Italians, Poles, Spaniards, and it has important Maghrebi and Sephardic communities and a strong African presence. The Rue Dejean market in Chateau Rouge, renowned as the market "of five continents," wants to move outside the walls (or rather beyond the *periferique*), and today is an important African commercial center in Europe, with merchandise coming from all over the continent. All around there are shops for music and videos from central Africa, Senegalese tailors and artisans, sellers of perfumed *tchurai*, a mixture of resin and perfume, much beloved by the women of central Africa. And above all hairdressers and sellers of hair products for the fabulous heads of hair of African ladies. All of this has the atmosphere of the street and the souk. This atmosphere also floats around the Tati chain of stores, which in Paris stands for the wide distribution of low-cost clothing and fabrics. All this is a world that doesn't belong to just the immigrant population of Paris but also to that of the general population, with sellers of materials and buttons, and stalls of remnants and trimmings. A strange part of Paris, often considered disaffiliated from those who are part of it, it also puts in question the paradoxical and ambiguous connection that the city has with the world. A place where constant comparison with an otherness perceived as "uncontrollable" brings out the difficulties and paradoxes that cross the slightly schizophrenic city that wants to please (almost) everyone but also to *monter en gamme* (go upmarket).[2] Because even the trend toward *mixité* is fine, so long as it remains as discreet as possible. Otherwise it becomes a "sensitive" question, as is demonstrated by the constant presence of the police at Chateau Rouge.

For decades this area of Paris has been the true filter for new arrivals, who find refuge there in a community close to their own origins. It's also the Paris that is still a little bohemian, where intellectuals and artists, new-generation designers, and restaurateurs with inventive ideas are still in residence. The municipality is always less welcoming to an experiment, in which they see the opposite of what they were proclaiming, a Paris where the settled communities would be invisible, as integrated and Frenchified as possible. If in the early years of the second millennium *mixité* has begun to be talked about, it is because the trend had arrived even in Paris, the idea of a multi-ethnic and multicolored city. But the trend passed rapidly from the heads of the administrators and local planners to be replaced by the "problem" of security and control. Chateau Rouge has always been under the eye of the police, who often run round-ups there, and the district has been one of the centers of resistance of the *sans papiers* (undocumented). Piero Zanini has lived there and has studied the happenings in the field, with Alessia de Biase, who directs the Laboratoire Architecture Anthropologie at the École Nationale Supérieure d'Architecture de Paris–La Villette. The surrounding city was the place to compare past and present and to question the signs of the future linked to the ongoing urban transformation processes, started in the early eighties and relaunched on a metropolitan scale after the recent international "consultation" for greater Paris, mandated by Sarkozy. There, where Paris is "renewing" itself by following increasingly paradoxical tendencies from the planning point of view: for example, designing entire quarters as if they were catalogs of architectural style (Clichy-Batignolles) or worse, issuing defining guidelines full of petty details that strictly limit the work of the planners, regulating everything that can possibly be regulated, that is, what happens on the ground floors and at street level. One has only to take a turn around any of the major expansions of the middle-class areas of the city, that thirteenth *arrondissement*, along the Seine and around the National Library mandated by Mitterand, often cited as the model to follow for the expansion of the city. Strolling with Piero Zanini in the Pajol-Stalingrad district and having in hand the study by one of his researchers on the destiny of the *rez-de-chaussée*,[3] we were amazed to observe the almost total disappearance of shops that open out onto the sidewalk. Instead there are walls and gratings that give the surrounding buildings the appearance of minifortresses. The commercial spaces have been moved into *grands surfaces*, to big box stores and closed-off areas equipped for this. One is aware that the street itself is at war with these regulations, and the way in which the intimate, private part of the city expresses itself—always with more difficulty—is in conflict with the more public and commercial part. Because of the new Parisian security measures, any obstruction that people gathering make on the sidewalks and in the surrounding shops—above all if they are *exotiques*—is something to be avoided. Even the shop signs have to be as "de-ethnicized" as possible: enough already with the halal butcher and the *chicha* smoker, enough already with Bengalese or Hindi script. It is something dangerous that reminds one too much of the old character of districts like Barbes and Chateau Rouge (which, to be sure, also have their own problems). Just as in the nineteenth century the reformers found it necessary to rid the city of the *classes dangereuses*—to promote hygiene and public order—so today the same consumers are considered a population to be kept under control. In actual fact, it is not the consumers who are dangerous, but it is rather a certain manner of being a consumer that bothers the "aesthetic" plane, it is in a moral sense, of "decency" and "convenience" etc., which in a totally bizarre manner links together—with appropriate differences—those who go to the market at Chateau Rouge with those who are drinking outside the local trendy bar.

The police regulations are a source of panic in such "unmanageable" places as the Metro, from the point of view of control. They can hound down the street people and layabouts by eliminating benches so that they have nowhere to sit and may only lean. In the neighborhoods, however, it's a bit simpler: one need only find a planner already in line with police regulations. As Zanini says, the problem is that this vision is very confused. It's as much a matter of creeping fascistization of the space due to the desire to appear as a world city—in a provincial key—a brand city that offers tranquility and control to new "international" users whatever the difficulty, as much as to an incapacity of seeing itself as a multiethnic city, a real global city.

The city wants to become high-class, resembling . . . who knows what it wants to resemble, because if it did know, it would have to admit to no longer being a capital city.

NOTES

1   Franco La Cecla, *Jet-Lag* (Turin: Bollati Boringhieri, 2002).

2   Maria Anita Palumbo, "Figures de l'habiter, modes de negociations du pluralisme a Barbes. L'altérité comme condition quotidienne," *Lieux Communs: Les Cahiers du LAUA* (Langages, Actions Urbaines, Altérités–École Nationale Supérieure d'Architecture de Nantes), no. 12 (2009): 129–48. http://www.laa.archi.fr/IMG/pdf/lieux-communs-Palumbo.pdf.

3   Chloé Goutille, *Au Rez-de-chaussée de la ville: Urbanité et vie citadine dans la transformations du quartiers Pajol-Stalingrad*, École Nationale Supérieure d'Architecture de Paris–Belleville, 2014.

A Note on the Text

Raffaele Milani

WHAT ARE THE PARAMETERS FOR CITIES TODAY, IN THE era of globalization? Does there still exist an urban spirit that could give a sense of real life to the half of the world's population who live in an endless built environment? What form do the megalopoli take in an epoch when history has decided to eliminate rural culture? Franco La Cecla, who is an anthropologist of actions, of things, and of organisms, ponders these questions regarding the present and future of human destiny in the wake of Lévi-Strauss's teaching, searching for signs of communities in transformation, by means of tangible and intangible objects, of sensual experiences, of the world of taste and food as well as in the dense patterns that make up the organization of social life. The contemporary city as a human project, and at the same time with its real dehumanization, is like a cloud of relationships, representations, and actions, as well as of smells and tastes. The anthropologist penetrates it to examine its structure and evolution, its current being, and its displacement. A traveling cloud, which, analyzed particle by particle, shows the ghosts of human life, endless examples of work and social dreaming. La Cecla also describes and interprets the images and the objects of cities in a controversial but civilized manner, shining the spotlight on the betrayal of certain technical formulas that seek to give the appearance of solving the problems of human indigence, poverty, personal misery, and possessions. Against the

stratagem of the multinationals rises the desperate and digni-
fied plaint from the land of the poor, which the author cannot
fail to record, in terms of truth and history, with a richness of
documentation and hopeful practicality.

La Cecla also follows up on the outlooks of social critics
such as Bruno Latour and doesn't overlook the heterotopics of
Foucault. A researcher in the manner of Lévi-Strauss, he none-
theless immerses himself in the provocative ideas put forward
by Unni Wikan. In order to understand, we need to touch, to
smell, to see, to hear our objective, the city: the one that exists
and the one that is disappearing, the one that is historic, muti-
lated, humiliated, degraded, and the one retrieved from the
newly impoverished. And our author does indeed venture into
experience and instance; his scrutiny doesn't offer us theories. He wants to experience the commonplace as a means of
identification. In fact, it is through the most ordinary, obvious
things and behaviors that we can track down the extraordinary signs of the work of humanity in motion. As he did years
ago for star-studded architecture, the author now goes after
urban planning. He criticizes it as an abstract system of representation, along with all of its "scientific" solutions, in order
to understand the tricks of a new enslavement that, shifting
projects of sustainability and intelligence, turns its prospects
upside down by reducing everything to a domain of sensitiv-
ity and heart. Touching, feeling, experiencing the gestures of
living also means emphasizing the corporeality of individuals
and populations anesthetized by the web universe. Behind the
city there appears a central question on the nature of man and
universal humanity: like a crowd scene Ivan Illich's teachings
and his utopian vision are added in a congenial manner to the
system of rules developed by Lévi-Strauss. In this book we are
made aware of the critical overdevelopment of productivity
and of the myth of consumerism, pitted against the value of
the creative freedom of the poor, a possible driving force for a
rediscovered conviviality.

La Cecla is a passionate traveler on an educative mission in the living world. He practices a vision of anthropology through the soul of his narration: he deploys a power of investigation in a charming, mild manner, recounting stories of situations in different cities of the world, in terms of key ideas to be conserved and updated. These include the realities of eco-sustainability, the distribution of goods, the humanization of the environment, the struggle against exploitation and new world servitude, and the culture of food as a symbolic and material exchange. We can easily take it all in from this book on the city of the present and of the future. The various points of his orientation, centered substantially on the themes of speculation in raw materials, environmental catastrophe, and the global energy crisis are leavened with portraits of cities such as Jogjakarta, Fukuoka, Istanbul, Shanghai, Kuala Lumpur, Tashkent, Milan, Minsk, and Ragusa. A critical social and symbolic projected field arises from these examples: the return of the group as protagonist in the great social uprisings, the misunderstandings and the lost occasions for participation, misery, and productivity in the slums, the ritual of eating on the street, the battles of the pajama-wearers and the laundry-spreaders. In this text he brings to light the physical presence of millions of people in the streets in Cairo, in Istanbul, in Hong Kong, in an identification between masses and location, as well as the myopia of anthropology and urban planning, incapable, according to the author, of understanding the use which political corporeality makes of public space and, above all, of those anonymous nonplaces. Examples of active citizenship, which tell of staying in a place and not simply passing through, invite a new analytical perspective of human sciences, beyond the interpretation of mapping, percentages, calculations of probability, statistics, and beyond the deceit of formulas for urban prosperity. We must, according to La Cecla, take hold of the "resonance" of real-life experience in order to be able to observe the way of life of the people: it is an experience of everyday life to be shared, through a disengagement of oneself so as to gravitate into the lives of others. La Cecla, far removed from the financial city of a George Soros and the spectacular city of a Guy Debord, makes himself into a follower of the vocation dictated by Tim Ingold, a form of knowledge for disguise: "Anthropology is the philosophy which has the courage to live outside."

Based on these reflections, let's retrace the modalities of a popular, not specialized, vision of the nature of the built environment, and of how it is, how it should and could be, very far removed from the sanctioned fatalism of Rem Koolhaas. The base of the spirit of the city is the life of its inhabitants. What Le Cecla wants to bring to light in fact, through the "spirit of the city," is the citizens' questioning perception of the current forms of the city in expansion, where the senses become dispirited and humiliated from spatial voids, from the lack of the finite, from stylistic and environmental incongruities, from desolate, barren or insignificant areas, and, at the same time, from the futurism of the "architectural genius." Department stores and traces of viability are reminders of inventive rethinking by the inhabitants that result in the slums turning up as an improvised city. The spirit of the city on the other hand is more than two thousand years old, because its roots are grounded in the culture of the city, according to its description by Lewis Mumford: a human experiment in cohabitation, among market, craft, and art, in a dialectic of closeness and passages, long pathways and spaces, in a continual relationship between people and constructed objects: walls, facades, highs and lows, heights, bridges, and walkways. With the car and the industrialization of the city they have become dematerialized, turned into abstract places of residence. And now, in the postmodern global cities, where it seems we no longer have a need for the countryside or for nature, just "hubs of ubiquity as well as entryways to a dematerialized geography," the thing is even more evident. Here Google, Facebook, Amazon, and Twitter can be seen as the Four Horsemen of the Apocalypse. It's the end of the garden city and the beginning of auto-construction, in spite of the great strength of Architecture for Humanity. The slogans *smart cities, creative cities, resilient cities, open-source cities* underline the futility. They are the signal of the end of the city and the art of designing, on the part of humanity, its chosen place.

About the Authors

Born in Palermo in 1950, **Franco La Cecla** is a renowned anthropologist and architect. He has taught anthropology in many European and Italian cities such as Palermo, Venice, Verona, Paris, and Barcelona. He has worked as a consultant for the Renzo Piano Building Workshop and for Barcelona Regional. In 2005 he founded the Architecture Social Impact Assessment, ASIA, an agency that evaluates the social impact of architectural and city planning projects. In addition, he has created several documentaries, one of which, *In Altro Mare* (In Another Sea) won the Best Coastal Culture Film award at the 2010 San Francisco Ocean Film Festival. His book *Against Architecture* is an international best seller.

Translator **Mairin O'Mahony** was born in London, where she worked as an editor for thirteen years before moving to San Francisco. Her experience includes a wide variety of copywriting on subjects ranging from agriculture to finance to travel. She is a passionate Italophile, dividing her time between San Francisco and Italy.

Raffaele Milani teaches the history of aesthetics in the Philosophy Department of the University of Bologna. He is the author of many books including, most recently, *The Art of the City*.

ABOUT PM PRESS

PM Press is an independent, radical publisher of books and media to educate, entertain, and inspire. Founded in 2007 by a small group of people with decades of publishing, media, and organizing experience, PM Press amplifies the voices of radical authors, artists, and activists. Our aim is to deliver bold political ideas and vital stories to all walks of life and arm the dreamers to demand the impossible. We have sold millions of copies of our books, most often one at a time, face to face. We're old enough to know what we're doing and young enough to know what's at stake. Join us to create a better world.

PM Press
PO Box 23912
Oakland, CA 94623
www.pmpress.org

PM Press in Europe
europe@pmpress.org
www.pmpress.org.uk

FRIENDS OF PM PRESS

These are indisputably momentous times—the financial system is melting down globally and the Empire is stumbling. Now more than ever there is a vital need for radical ideas.

In the years since its founding—and on a mere shoestring—PM Press has risen to the formidable challenge of publishing and distributing knowledge and entertainment for the struggles ahead. With over 450 releases to date, we have published an impressive and stimulating array of literature, art, music, politics, and culture. Using every available medium, we've succeeded in connecting those hungry for ideas and information to those putting them into practice.

Friends of PM allows you to directly help impact, amplify, and revitalize the discourse and actions of radical writers, filmmakers, and artists. It provides us with a stable foundation from which we can build upon our early successes and provides a much-needed subsidy for the materials that can't necessarily pay their own way. You can help make that happen—and receive every new title automatically delivered to your door once a month—by joining as a Friend of PM Press. And, we'll throw in a free T-shirt when you sign up.

Here are your options:

- **$30 a month** Get all books and pamphlets plus 50% discount on all webstore purchases

- **$40 a month** Get all PM Press releases (including CDs and DVDs) plus 50% discount on all webstore purchases

- **$100 a month** Superstar—Everything plus PM merchandise, free downloads, and 50% discount on all webstore purchases

For those who can't afford $30 or more a month, we have **Sustainer Rates** at $15, $10 and $5. Sustainers get a free PM Press T-shirt and a 50% discount on all purchases from our website.

Your Visa or Mastercard will be billed once a month, until you tell us to stop. Or until our efforts succeed in bringing the revolution around. Or the financial meltdown of Capital makes plastic redundant. Whichever comes first.

Credo of The Green Arcade

The Green Arcade, a curated bookstore, specializes in sustainability, from the built environment to the natural world. The Green Arcade is a meeting place for rebels, flaneurs, farmers, and architects: those who build, inhabit, and add something valuable to the world.

The Green Arcade

1680 Market Street

San Francisco, CA 94102–5949

www.thegreenarcade.com

Against Architecture

Franco La Cecla
Translated by Mairin O'Mahony

ISBN: 978-1-60486-406-9
$14.95   144 pages

First published in 2008, (as *Contro
l'architettura*), *Against Architecture* has been
translated into French and Greek, with
editions forthcoming in Polish and Portuguese.
The book is a passionate and erudite charge
against the celebrities of the current architectural world, the "archistars."
According to Franco La Cecla, architecture has lost its way and its true
function, as the archistars use the cityscape to build their brand, putting
their stamp on the built environment with no regard for the public good.

More than a diatribe against the trade for which he trained, Franco La
Cecla issues a call to rethink urban space, to take our cities back from
what he calls Casino Capitalism, which has left a string of failed urban
projects, from the Sagrera of Barcelona to the expansion of Columbia
University in New York City. As he comments throughout on the works
of past and present masters of urban and landscape writing, including
Robert Byron, Mike Davis, and Rebecca Solnit, Franco La Cecla has given
us a book that will take an important place in our public discourse.

"To tell the truth, Franco La Cecla is not wrong. There is too much building,
sometimes only to put a signature, a stamp on a spot, without any worry
about the people who are going to live there. In other situations it is easy to
be used by the institutions that support speculation. It is the reason why I
refused many projects, because, I am lucky—and I can choose."
— Renzo Piano in *La Repubblica*

"La Cecla's book is a delight, in the way that he dismantles the glory of the
'archistar' in their proud myopic grandeur that totally ignores people and
their rights to a better urban life."
— Sebastian Courtois, *La Reforme*

Pictures of a Gone City: Tech and the Dark Side of Prosperity in the San Francisco Bay Area

Richard A. Walker

ISBN: 978-1-62963-510-1
$26.95   480 pages

The San Francisco Bay Area is currently the jewel in the crown of capitalism—the tech capital of the world and a gusher of wealth from the Silicon Gold Rush. It has been generating jobs, spawning new innovation, and spreading ideas that are changing lives everywhere. It boasts of being the Left Coast, the Greenest City, and the best place for workers in the USA. So what could be wrong? It may seem that the Bay Area has the best of it in Trump's America, but there is a dark side of success: overheated bubbles and spectacular crashes; exploding inequality and millions of underpaid workers; a boiling housing crisis, mass displacement, and severe environmental damage; a delusional tech elite and complicity with the worst in American politics.

This sweeping account of the Bay Area in the age of the tech boom covers many bases. It begins with the phenomenal concentration of IT in Greater Silicon Valley, the fabulous economic growth of the bay region and the unbelievable wealth piling up for the 1% and high incomes of Upper Classes—in contrast to the fate of the working class and people of color earning poverty wages and struggling to keep their heads above water. The middle chapters survey the urban scene, including the greatest housing bubble in the United States, a metropolis exploding in every direction, and a geography turned inside out. Lastly, it hits the environmental impact of the boom, the fantastical ideology of Tech World, and the political implications of the tech-led transformation of the bay region.

"With Pictures of a Gone City, *California's greatest geographer tells us how the Bay Area has become the global center of hi-tech capitalism. Drawing on a lifetime of research, Richard Walker dismantles the mythology of the New Economy, placing its creativity in a long history of power, work, and struggles for justice."*
—Jason W. Moore, author of *Capitalism in the Web of Life*

The City Is Ours: Squatting and Autonomous Movements in Europe from the 1970s to the Present

Edited by Bart van der Steen, Ask Katzeff, and Leendert van Hoogenhuijze with a Preface by George Katsiaficas and Foreword by Geronimo

ISBN: 978-1-60486-683-4
$21.95   336 pages

Squatters and autonomous movements have been in the forefront of radical politics in Europe for nearly a half-century—from struggles against urban renewal and gentrification, to large-scale peace and environmental campaigns, to spearheading the antiausterity protests sweeping the continent.

Through the compilation of the local movement histories of eight different cities—including Amsterdam, Berlin, and other famous centers of autonomous insurgence along with underdocumented cities such as Poznan and Athens—*The City Is Ours* paints a broad and complex picture of Europe's squatting and autonomous movements.

Each chapter focuses on one city and provides a clear chronological narrative and analysis accompanied by photographs and illustrations. The chapters focus on the most important events and developments in the history of these movements. Furthermore, they identify the specificities of the local movements and deal with issues such as the relation between politics and subculture, generational shifts, the role of confrontation and violence, and changes in political tactics.

All chapters are written by politically-engaged authors who combine academic scrutiny with accessible writing. Readers with an interest in the history of the newest social movements will find plenty to mull over here. Contributors include Nazima Kadir, Gregor Kritidis, Claudio Cattaneo, Enrique Tudela, Alex Vasudevan, Needle Collective and the Bash Street Kids, René Karpantschof, Flemming Mikkelsen, Lucy Finchett-Maddock, Grzegorz Piotrowski, and Robert Foltin.

The Housing Monster

Prole.info

ISBN: 978-1-60486-530-1
$14.95   160 pages

The Housing Monster is a scathing illustrated essay that takes one seemingly simple, everyday thing—a house—and looks at the social relations that surround it. Moving from intensely personal thoughts and interactions to large-scale political and economic forces, it reads alternately like a worker's diary, a short story, a psychology of everyday life, a historical account, an introduction to Marxist critique of political economy, and an angry flyer someone would pass you on the street.

Starting with the construction site and the physical building of houses, the book slowly builds and links more and more issues together: from gentrification and city politics to gender roles and identity politics, from subcontracting and speculation to union contracts and negotiation, from individual belief, suffering, and resistance to structural division, necessity, and instability. What starts as a look at housing broadens into a critique of capitalism as a whole. The text is accompanied by clean black-and-white illustrations that are mocking, beautiful, and bleak.

"*A thorough and easy-to-read analysis of the fight at the construction site and what the conditions are for the struggle in the city and for the land.*"
—Kämpa Tillsammans!

"*Part illustrated guide to Marx, part analysis of the everyday consequences of producing and consuming housing as a commodity, and part revolutionary call to arms!*"
—Aufheben

"*Looking for a place to dwell? Or even for an entirely new world to live in? But maybe you're afraid radical theory is boring? Then* The Housing Monster *is the book for you. The author of the now classic* Abolish Restaurants *has come to grips with another vital issue: the housing question. Class analysis + a critique of daily life + uncensored innovative graphics + more. . . Enjoy!*"
—Gilles Dauvé

Re-enchanting the World: Feminism and the Politics of the Commons

Silvia Federici
with a Foreword by Peter Linebaugh

ISBN: 978-1-62963-569-9
$19.95   240 pages

Silvia Federici is one of the most important contemporary theorists of capitalism and feminist movements. In this collection of her work spanning over twenty years, she provides a detailed history and critique of the politics of the commons from a feminist perspective. In her clear and combative voice, Federici provides readers with an analysis of some of the key issues and debates in contemporary thinking on this subject.

Drawing on rich historical research, she maps the connections between the previous forms of enclosure that occurred with the birth of capitalism and the destruction of the commons and the "new enclosures" at the heart of the present phase of global capitalist accumulation. Considering the commons from a feminist perspective, this collection centers on women and reproductive work as crucial to both our economic survival and the construction of a world free from the hierarchies and divisions capital has planted in the body of the world proletariat. Federici is clear that the commons should not be understood as happy islands in a sea of exploitative relations but rather autonomous spaces from which to challenge the existing capitalist organization of life and labor.

"Silvia Federici's theoretical capacity to articulate the plurality that fuels the contemporary movement of women in struggle provides a true toolbox for building bridges between different features and different people."
—Massimo De Angelis, professor of political economy, University of East London

"Silvia Federici's work embodies an energy that urges us to rejuvenate struggles against all types of exploitation and, precisely for that reason, her work produces a common: a common sense of the dissidence that creates a community in struggle."
—Maria Mies, coauthor of *Ecofeminism*